SHOE TOWN

SHOE TOWN

Rodney Lee

Ambassador Books, Inc.
Worcester • Massachusetts

Library of Congress Cataloging-in-Publication Data

Lee, Rodney, 1945-
  Shoe town / Rodney Lee.
      p. cm.
  Includes index.
  ISBN 1-929039-27-1 (hardcover)
  1. Lee, Rodney, 1945---Childhood and youth. 2. Family--New York (State)--Endicott--History--20th century. 3. Football--Social aspects--New York (State)--Endicott--History--20th century. 4. Company towns--New York (State)--Endicott--History--20th century. 5. Shoe industry--New York (State)--Endicott--History--20th century. 6. Endicott (N.Y.)--Social life and customs--20th century. 7. Endicott (N.Y.)--Biography. 8. Endicott (N.Y.)--Economic conditions--20th century. I. Title.

  F129.E7L44 2004
  974.7'75'0092--dc22

                          2004017836

Published in the United States by Ambassador Books, Inc.
91 Prescott Street, Worcester, Massachusetts 01605
(800) 577-0909

Printed in the United States.
For current information about all titles from Ambassador Books, Inc.,
visit our website at: www.ambassadorbooks.com.

Jacket Design by Vision Advertising, Worcester, Massachusetts

To Horace Lee Jr. (*posthumously*)
and Beatrice Mae (*Blossom*) Lee,
who gave so much
—*asking so little in return.*

ACKNOWLEDGEMENTS

The development of Shoe Town was aided in considerable measure by the assistance of a number of people, including my wife, Marie, of Linwood, Massachusetts, my daughters Caroline (also of Linwood) and Amanda, of Oxford, Massachusetts, Christine Froio of Charlton, Massachusetts and Dick Broszeit of Shrewsbury, Massachusetts—all of whom proofed portions of the text and offered constructive criticism.

I am also grateful to Coach Fran Angeline (retired) and to Judy Welch and Al Brunetti of Union-Endicott High School in Endicott, New York, for their enthusiastic support.

I owe Laura DiBenedetto of Vision Advertising, in Worcester, Massachusetts, a hearty thank you for her stellar work in bringing the cover and other "outside elements" of Shoe Town to life. And to Jennifer Conlan of Ambassador Books in Worcester, Massachusetts, for her diligent attention to detail in the set-up of the book.

I am indebted to the publishers and authors of the following books, all of which predated my own and which proved invaluable as I researched events, dates, places and names: A History of the

Town of Union and *A History of Endicott* (by the late James V. Fiori); *The Valley of Opportunity/A Pictorial History of the Greater Binghamton Area* (by Gerald R. Smith); *Partners All* (produced by the Huntington Corp., with photographs by Russell C. Atkins); and *This Tiger's Tale*, by Coach Angeline.

Last but certainly not least comes my cousin Joyce (Turner) More of Endicott, New York, who believed in the premise of *Shoe Town* from the outset. Joyce provided reams of background material. She expressed unflagging interest as the work progressed. Her encouragement carried me forward and helped me complete the project.

Table of Contents

Foreword. 11

Introduction 13

   I. "The Magic City" 23

  II. Trouble in Paradise 29

 III. West Corners Comes of Age 37

 IV. An Arch for "George F." 49

  V. Our "Field of Dreams". 59

 VI. A Rude Awakening. 67

 VII. Gasping for Breath. 73

VIII. "Cy," Courtship & Cider 85

 IX. A "Welcome" from "Coach Nick". 93

  X. A New Era Dawns. 99

 XI. Together on "The Avenue" 105

 XII. Rockin' & Rollin' 111

XIII. The Pig Stand—and a Loss 117

XIV. Agony and Ecstacy 125

 XV. A Rivalry Catches Fire 137

XVI. Stung by the Green Hornets 147

XVII. On the Road Again. 157

XVIII. Mentors and "Devils" 167

XIX. The Tiger Growls Again 181

 XX. "Fran the Man". 187

XXI. Round and Round We Go 201

XXII. "I Prouda I Endicott" 209

XXIII. "Which Way E-J?". 219

Epilogue 226

Index 236

FOREWORD

One of the memorable scenes in the 1973 Sydney Pollack romance film *The Way We Were* occurs near the end of the movie; Hollywood screenwriter Hubell Gardner (Robert Redford) and his best friend J.J. (Bradford Dillman) are alone on a yacht, swilling beers. The boat is skimming serenely across the surface of the water, at full sail. Continuing a tradition that is a carryover from their college days, Hubell and J.J. reach deep (deeper than necessary, considering the trivial nature of the subject matter) to supply one another with the answer to such recurring-but-inconsequential questions as "best bourbon?," "best weather report?," "best Saturday afternoon?" and "best month?"

When J.J. gets to "best year?," Hubell, suddenly misty-eyed and obviously thinking of the only woman he has truly loved, and who is slipping through his fingers for good (the exasperatingly liberal political and social crusader Katie Morosky Gardner, portrayed by Barbra Streisand), replies, " '44. . . no, '45. . . '46. . ."

Looking back, we all treasure those moments that define our lives. Such a time for me came in the summer and early fall of 1960. I was fourteen. My passion for sports and Rock 'N' Roll was exceeded only by my newfound infatuation with "babes." I was

11

rapturously involved with a smolderingly beautiful and sultry classmate. I was getting ready to enter Union-Endicott High School, in the small upstate New York village of Endicott, as a sophomore. I was a budding basketball player with what by all indications appeared to be a bright future in the game.

Coincidentally, a native son and esteemed U-E alum was due to return to the school as its new football coach. An entire community was certain that Francis J. "Fran" Angeline would reawaken the beast in the Tigers, whose roar had been reduced to a meow.

A boy my age could not have dreamed of better circumstances. I was deliriously happy. "Shoe Town, U.S.A.," home of the Endicott-Johnson Corp., which employed thousands of people (including my paternal grandparents), had provided our village with riches beyond compare. My grandparents lived in an "E-J" house they had purchased from the company. I attended a church that had grown in size and stature with E-J's help. I swam in a pool E-J had built. I rode a wooden carousel in a park E-J had created. I bought pastries and movie tickets and records and sporting goods in a shopping district that was a direct outgrowth of E-J's ascendancy.

Self-absorbed and without a care, I was totally unaware that my hometown was dying. Or that my own idyllic existence was about to be jarred by setbacks I had not seen coming.

I was oblivious to troubling questions that hung in the air like thunderclouds.

Could E-J survive the escalating cost of doing business and the threat of snazzier products manufactured by its rivals?

Could "The Avenue" withstand the twin hammer blows of a shrinking local work force and the imminent arrival of the area's first mall?

Could U-E High School's football program recapture its brilliance?

Was my teenage romance about to crash on the rocks?

Could I emerge as U-E's next great "cager?"

Was the world I'd known about to crumble in my hands?

INTRODUCTION

R oll the calendar back to the year 1960, one of the most pivotal in American history. The country was on the cusp of great change. In November, a magnetic young Democrat from Massachusetts—John F. Kennedy—would defeat Richard M. Nixon by a razor-thin plurality to become the youngest man elected president, and the first Catholic to gain the office. Three years later, JFK was dead: assassinated in Dallas on November 23rd, 1963 at the age of forty-six. My roommate and I heard the news on the radio that sat on the window sill of our room in a dormitory at Fredonia State College in Fredonia, New York, on an otherwise exquisitely serene and sun-dashed autumn afternoon. Camelot had come crashing down. In its place arrived continuing upheaval through the rest of the decade: the assassinations of Robert F. Kennedy and Martin Luther King, Jr.; racial protests and race riots; the Vietnam War; demonstrations that ripped the country asunder; the rise of a counterculture whose leaders preached dissent bordering on revolution; Woodstock.

The early months of 1960 in my hometown of Endicott, New York—equidistant between New York City and Buffalo, on the Susquehanna River—offered few clues that a state of mayhem was about to descend on the U.S. like a plague, or that the turbulent times to follow would inflict wounds on the national psyche that would remain as open sores for many years afterwards. Dwight D. Eisenhower—"Ike," the military hero who had proven to be a good shepherd during the relatively benign 1950's—was still president and enjoying tremendous popularity in Republican strongholds of the nation like Broome County. In Endicott, as elsewhere, the Age of Innocence had not yet given way to the Age of Disenchantment and Disillusion.

Like other fourteen-year-olds growing up in Endicott in 1960, I was ensconced in a virtual Utopia. What could possibly be wrong? Who could have it better than me? I had many reasons to feel content and secure:

In January of 1960, a feel-good movie—A *Summer Place*, starring Richard Egan, Dorothy McGuire, Sandra Dee, Arthur Kennedy and Troy Donahue—was playing at the Elvin, in Union. . .

That same month, tickets were selling fast for a Saturday-night sock hop at the recreation hall in nearby Johnson City. The dance was being hosted by local radio DJ's Bob Richards and Joe Julian and would feature the pop-group "Bobby and the Counts;" "Rock 'N' Roll" had hit the nation head-on, and I reveled in the commotion it was causing. . .

Several mornings a week, a milkman from Magic City Ice Co. delivered milk and orange juice—in sturdy, narrow-necked glass bottles—to the doorstep of our home. . .

The *Endicott Daily Bulletin*, a mere five cents and brimming with local news, arrived at our doorstep each afternoon. . .

On Friday evenings my mom came home from work toting large sheets of Roma's pizza. . .

The radio was almost always tuned to WENE ("Wee-Nee," 1430 on the dial). . .

Steamed pork-barbecue sandwiches layered with sweet relish, all the rage, were delivered by "car hops" straight to the rolled-down windows of automobiles parked in front of Grover's Pig Stand, in Endwell. . .

On warm summer nights crowds queued up outside Pat Mitchell's for homemade ice cream that slid down the throat like maple syrup. . .

The New York Yankees would soon be heading south for spring training and their Eastern League farm team (our very own Binghamton Triplets) would be starting their season. . .

My favorite show, the TV-western "Death Valley Days," featuring the "Old Ranger" and sponsored by U.S. Borax, was a staple of the programming line-up on WNBF (Channel 12 on our black-and-white set). . .

There were no area codes; telephone numbers had a romantic ring to them, consisting of letters and numbers, as in ST(for Stillwell)5-3355.

It was as if I had fingered my way through a mail-order catalog, stopped on the page depicting scruffy sandlots, corner candy stores like Duffy's (in West Corners), creek beds like the Nanticoke (great for catching minnows and frogs), rivers like the Susquehanna (an ideal place to fish for bullhead and carp), forested hillsides like "Round Top" (which housed hidden caves and buried Indian arrowheads) and oodles of friends and family and said: "I want that. . . 'The Perfect Life.' "

Alone in my bedroom, I dreamed of making love to Mamie Van Doren, the statuesque and gorgeous blonde bombshell appearing in the film *Girls Town*; soon, realizing that Van Doren was out of my reach, I shifted my attention to the black-haired beauty, about my age, who'd recently moved into the new brick house across the street: Marie Sergi, daughter of "Sam the Barber." I'd watch "Sergi" sunning herself in her yard from my bedroom window. I secretly pined for her even though I was already "involved" with an Italian siren from West Endicott. Sexual urges were running strong, and I had no desire to suppress them.

— ❖ —

In Endicott in 1960, little evidence existed that "The Space Age" and incredible technological advances were on the horizon. International Business Machines (IBM), which had gotten its start in Endicott, was already building computers in the firm's manufacturing plants on North Street, but in countless other ways the rhythms of village life were not much different than the ones my parents had become accustomed to during the early years of their marriage. Endicott was a blue-collar community, built by immigrants. Members of my own family labored with their hands. My grandfather on my mother's side—James F. "Jim" Blossom— had been a tradesman, specializing in masonry, until his retirement. I was told he built the best fireplaces around (the one in his home, in Apalachin, worked like a charm). My maternal grandmother, Blanche Blossom, maintained a spacious house and a large garden; she also worked part-time as a cleaning woman. My paternal grandparents, Horace and Lillian Lee, had both worked in the factories of the Endicott-Johnson Shoe and Tanning Company. An uncle—Robert E. Charlesworth Stanton Lee ("Bob" Lee for short)—owned a mill that built garage doors and windows. His younger brothers—my father, Horace Lee Jr., Ray and Stew—were all carpenters.

The activities that constituted my life in 1960 occurred within a short distance of my home. I played baseball, basketball and football on the fields and courts of the West Corners Elementary School, less than a mile from my house—in a neighborhood, slightly northwest of the village's center, that was just starting to spread its wings. I shopped with my mom and went to the movies in Union, four miles away, or on Washington Avenue in Endicott, about six miles distant. I attended religious services at the West Endicott Baptist Church. I often spent weekends at my grandparent Lees' house in West Endicott or my grandparent Blossoms' house in Apalachin. I spent my free time at West Endicott Park, a few blocks from my grandparent Lees' house, or traipsing around West Corners, West Endicott and Endicott.

I seldom ventured beyond a radius of several miles. I reached most of my destinations by bicycle. Sometimes I hitchhiked; sticking one's thumb in the air for a ride was a respectable way of getting around, and adults I knew ("Rollie" Colvin, "Red" Wood, Joyce Mitchell, "Dick" Herman and others) were happy to give me a lift.

I came from a large family. My dad was one of eleven children, my mom one of four. I had two younger brothers.

I did not lack for friends.

Whenever the family gathered, the conversation inevitably got around to Endicott-Johnson and its co-founder, George F. Johnson, who had died in 1948. To hear my grandparents, my mom and dad and my other relatives tell it, "George F." was the be all and end all when it came to employers. They were not alone in this sentiment; any mention of Endicott's rise to prominence by my teachers, when they touched on local history, was sure to include a reference to Johnson and the enormous contributions made by E-J as the village grew from a quiet agricultural and lumbering community to a manufacturing hubbub.

By the age of fourteen, I was well aware of two monuments to George F. Johnson. One was a soaring concrete arch on Main Street. The arch served as the gateway to Endicott from the village's sister town of Union. It bore the inscription "Home of the Square Deal." A little farther east on Main Street, between the high school and E-J's executive offices, a handsome bronze statue of Johnson had been erected.

These were the two most conspicuous physical symbols of villagers' affection for George F. Johnson. A community's gratitude did not end there, however. No one I knew was shy when it came to expressing love and respect for the "pioneer" whose shoe company had put Endicott on the map and whose generosity toward the workingman and workingwoman was a matter of record.

It had taken a couple of "Yankees" from Massachusetts, Henry B. Endicott and George F. Johnson, to build the shoe company that bore their name, and to create the village in which I was raised. Their lots had been cast together in the 1890's at the Lester brothers' shoe factory just up the road in the city of Binghamton. Endicott, an astute businessman, was the company's treasurer. Johnson was a foreman. Endicott had invested considerable sums of money in an attempt to keep the Lester brothers' operation, which was floundering, solvent; Johnson, several years younger than his peer, had demonstrated prowess in a supervisory position. By 1900 Johnson had also developed a financial stake in the firm and was urging Endicott to set up a new shoe company on flat agricultural and farming land several miles west. It was the ideal location, Johnson felt, to bring to fruition his own vision of a community in which management and labor would live and work side by side, in absolute harmony. The deal was sealed. The Endicott-Johnson Shoe and Tanning Company was spawned. With it came establishment of the village of Endicott, which was incorporated in 1906, and a commercial district (Washington Avenue) that instantly drew shoppers from miles in every direction.

With the founding of the village came the start of a high school, Union-Endicott, and the eventual arrival there, in the late 1940's, of a football player named Fran Angeline whose rugged good looks were complemented by enormous talent and a searing passion for the game. Angeline starred at U-E and at Colgate University. In the fall of 1960, at the still tender age of twenty-five, he returned to his alma mater to take charge of a football program that had become the laughingstock of the conference. He retired thirty-two seasons later as the winningest coach in "Triple Cities" history.

Endicott, and Union-Endicott High School, might not have come into being at all were it not for Endicott-Johnson.

— ❖ —

When Endicott-Johnson cut back its production in the late 1960's and began yanking most of its workforce out of Endicott, the village was suddenly like a ship without a rudder. Despite the continuing presence of IBM, the community was adrift in the open sea—tossing helplessly as it tried to get its bearings. Washington Avenue, the success of which had been so interconnected to E-J's, had already begun to lose storefronts and customers. The departure of E-J accelerated the demise of "The Avenue." Other symbols of "the E-J years" started to disappear. The most prominent of these, En-Joie Park, a vast, sprawling domain featuring a pavilion, picnic tables, a carousel and a gargantuan swimming pool, slipped into neglect and ultimately vanished altogether. The loss of En-Joie Park was a catastrophic blow to the village's pride. It would, unfortunately, not be the last.

"The E-J years" lasted less than a century in Endicott, but their impact continues to be felt. It is, in fact, ingrained in the very soil of the village. This is true despite the fact that much of the evidence that Endicott-Johnson even once existed is now gone. Most of E-J's factory buildings were demolished many years ago. Some of the other properties that the Johnson family developed for the benefit of the community—like Ideal Hospital on "Round Hill," or "Round Top," in West Endicott (high above the Susquehanna, with a view of the river looking east), where I was born and which was later turned into an old-folks home—have "changed their stripes" from their initial purpose, so to speak.

The lasting legacy of the E-J era can never be lost, however, so long as the particulars of the company's accomplishments and its benevolence toward all residents of the village are remembered.

In 1937, in a pictorial-narrative book entitled *Partners All* that was produced by the Huntington Corporation and that featured riveting workplace photographs by Russell C. Aikins, Endicott-Johnson was referred to as "an industrial democracy." Others have identified E-J's approach to doing business as "paternalistic capitalism." These descriptions are most appropriate; they reflect

George F. Johnson's belief that E-J's workers were not to be viewed as employees but rather as "partners" in "a common enterprise." Johnson's conviction that fair wages for a fair day's work should be company policy never wavered. This is why, at the peak of "labor warfare" in the Midwest in the winter of '37, virtually all of E-J's tanners, shoemakers and rubber workers signed a pledge of their "loyalty and goodwill" and "complete confidence" in the leadership of the Johnsons. It's why, at E-J, workers earned wages that were 20% to 30% higher than at other shoe-manufacturing plants in the U.S. It's why E-J workers paid out of their own pockets for the construction of the arch straddling Main Street on the Union/Endicott line as a tribute to Johnson; the arch was dedicated, fittingly enough, on Labor Day (in 1920). It's why the Triple Cities came to be known as "the Home of the Square Deal" and "the Valley of Opportunity." It's why Johnson's motto that E-J would "live and help live"—a variation of the famous expression "live and let live"—was heartily endorsed by his workers. It's why to this day no one in Endicott speaks of George F. Johnson except in the most glowing terms.

Shoe Town is an account of the rise and fall of the village of Endicott, New York; a lament, if you will. It is set in a year—1960—in which E-J was on its way out and the village's most flamboyant and illustrious high school football coach, "Fran the Man" Angeline, was on his way in: destinies converging. It is a story about factories, families and football. The names, places and dates have not been changed. I came to the conclusion, during the course of writing this book, that the people who have emerged as the main characters are far too interesting to be portrayed as anyone but their real selves. And so *Shoe Town* evolved as a work of non-fiction.

Shoe Town is a true story.

R.L.
Linwood, Massachusetts
September, 2004

Well I was born in a small town
And I live in a small town
Prob'ly die in a small town
Oh, those small communities

All my friends are so small town
My parents live in the same small town
My job is so small town
Provides little opportunity

— John Mellencamp, "Small Town"

"Glory days, they'll pass you by
in the wink of a young girl's eye. . . "

— Bruce Springsteen, "Glory Days"

Endicott's Washington Avenue, circa 1935.

"The Magic City"

I t never occurred to me, when I was fourteen, that my grandfather would stop dancing. Or that I would be anything less
than the best athlete on the block or that my hometown of
Endicott, New York, would fall to such ruin that I would cringe
in embarrassment, years later, at the mere thought of returning
from Massachusetts for a visit.

It did not cross my mind that all of this would happen in a
flash; that within the blink of an eye Grampa Lee would be gone
and the world I had known would break into smithereens, like
Humpty Dumpty. I was about to run head-on into disappointment of the most profound kind; punctuated, as if a dagger were
being driven into my heart, by the collapse of the manufacturing
dynasty upon which our very subsistence was grounded.

Endicott was known locally as "The Magic City." During my
boyhood, in the 1950's and 1960's, it was easy to see why. There
was nothing to dislike about the village. It was, in fact, the envy
of nearby communities for its many assets: wide, genteel, tree-
lined streets, many of which were named after presidents

(Lincoln, Jefferson, Roosevelt, Washington, Monroe, Garfield, Madison, etc.); parks and playgrounds and ball fields everywhere one turned; a busy train station; a boy's club; a small but active airport on the outskirts of town; and more stores and theaters than any community had a right to call its own.

I had come to take for granted all of the embellishments that were a staple of life in Endicott back then, never suspecting that other kids in other places did not enjoy the same privileged circumstances. I should have known better. It should have been obvious to me that nearby communities' endowments were not nearly as impressive as Endicott's, but I did not spend much time dwelling on this disparity. Besides, neighboring cities and towns held an attraction all their own. Owego, to our west, was interesting for the "old" look and feel of its inner core of homes and businesses; interesting, too, because some of its downtown storefronts literally backed up to the river. Johnson City and Binghamton, to our east, teemed with commercial activity. Binghamton was the first actual city with which I came into contact: an intriguing place, where murder and mayhem were not all that infrequent an occurrence.

My journey through adolescence had been a joyride. Except for a fistfight with a school bully that occurred in the seventh grade and a brief, comical attempt to help a friend organize a gang the next year, I had breezed through Jennie F. Snapp Junior High School without causing a ripple of notice.

The slugfest had erupted spontaneously in a cloakroom; it was ancient history by the time I had licked my wounds and returned to Mrs. (Mary) Loomis' homeroom the next morning. The initial confrontation had lasted only a few seconds. The continuation didn't last much longer. It took place in a wide-open, black-topped area in back of the school, and drew a High Noon-like crowd of our bloodthirsty classmates to the scene. I was shocked at the size of the gathering. The fifty or so onlookers seemed to come out of nowhere. They quickly formed a circle around us, hemming us in. They had barely begun yelling encouragement to the combatant they'd selected as their warrior of choice when the principal, Martin Bortnick, Jr., rushed to the center of the ring, hauling my tormentor and me by the scruff of our necks to his office for a tongue-lashing. It was an inglorious finish to what everyone present was certain would be "the Clash of the Century."

A tall, no-nonsense man who wore glasses, Mr. Bortnick must have thought to himself as he dismissed us, "I won't have any trouble remembering these two: they're both named Rodney!"

The unoriginal moniker Richard Havich and I had selected for the band of hoodlums we tried to put together the following fall— "The Rebels"—probably explains why the undertaking did not generate the sense of dread in my mother that I had hoped it would; she simply smiled when we started wearing loud black and red-striped leather jackets. She shrugged in unconcerned resignation when we began meeting clandestinely at Dick's house on No. Nanticoke Avenue in West Endicott, "to scheme." She had even taken me to the basement of Vaughn's, a clothing store in Union (she purchased all of her sons' attire there then), so that I could buy the jacket I had told her was the one I wanted for my walk on the wild side.

By applying gobs of Wildroot to our hair, rolling up the sleeves of our T-shirts to the shoulders, slipping into tight-fitting "pegged" pants and puckering our lips, Dick Havich and I managed to approximate the James Dean look: diffident; disenfranchised; "cool." When our get-ups prompted only guffaws of derision from acquaintances instead of fresh recruits for our prospective pack of juvenile delinquents, Dick and I, chagrined, chose the same course any weak-kneed excuse for a mobster would follow: we packed it in. My career as a thug on the order of a Machine Gun Kelly, Babyface Nelson or Tony Soprano lasted no more than a month. Thankfully for the two of us—if not for our prospective "victims"—it never reached the brass knuckles, chains and switchblades stage.

Aside from these aberrational moments, I was a model son and above-average student, and a genuine star on the sandlots and basketball courts around town. I was the envy of the younger kids in West Corners for my prowess at sports, and a big shot with my cronies for having won the charms of an alluring and foxy fellow ninth grader. Laurene Perfetti, who came from respectable, sturdy Italian-American stock, was a definite "catch." In West Endicott, Union and Endicott, where we hung out, Laurene and I were an item. We probed the first stirrings of sexual arousal on the couch in Laurene's living room on weekday afternoons—our eagerness for necking emboldened that much more when her parents weren't home and her brother Tony wasn't looking. We kissed and caressed with near-total abandon. Lust throbbed in our veins.

Laurene and I had completed our studies at Jennie F. Snapp Junior High School and were poised to make the leap to Union-Endicott High School.

We would make that jump together, with our friends. Nothing was going to change certain givens. Not even a stark new environment.

Life was good.

I had not witnessed or experienced real trouble.

I was encased in the cocoon of protection my dad, a carpenter, and my mom—a receptionist, secretary, bookkeeper and homemaker—had built around me.

It was the summer of 1960.

Endicott had provided me with a bountiful youth, full of adventure and activity. I was dizzily riding the wheel of fortune as it spun on its axis—certain that it would never stop.

Things were only going to get better.

I was very naïve.

My grandmother's birthday is celebrated with a family photo in the early 1950's. Front Row, from the left: (brother) Roger Lee; (cousin) Nancy Lee; (cousin) Roberta Lee; (cousin) Jack Lee; (the author) Rodney Lee; (cousin) Sharon Lee; (cousin) Pam Cornell; (cousin) Gary Lee; (brother) Richard Lee. Middle Row: my Aunt Margaret; my cousin Sandra; unidentified airman; (Gram) Lillian Lee; (cousin) Carol (Turner) Cornell's husband Lloyd; Grandpa Lee; (cousin) Carol Cornell; (cousin) Joyce Turner; Back Row: (Aunt) Honey Lee; (mom) Beatrice Lee; (dad) Horace Lee Jr.; (Aunt) Alberta Lee; (Uncle) Bob Lee; (Uncle) "Bun" Turner; (Aunt) Harriet Turner; (Uncle) Stewart Lee; (cousin) Larry Lee with (Uncle) Ray and (Aunt) Hazel Lee; (cousin) Bobby Lee; Teresa Frgundorfer; Joan Cornell.

TROUBLE IN PARADISE

As we gathered on Grampa Lee's lawn in West Endicott that July for the annual cookout that doubled as his birthday party and a family reunion, I was certain that no yard could be more beautiful. There would be, in due course, exposure to green-er pastures: the lush fairways of Oak Hill Country Club in Rochester (site of golf's 1968 U.S. Open, which I attended as a sportswriter) and the manicured lawns that fronted the mansions on Ocean Drive in Newport, to name two. Back then, however, my grandfather's narrow but deep side yard, stretching one hun-dred fifty feet from the sidewalk bordering Jennings Street to the rear bounds of the property, was, without question, the fairest piece of turf to be found for miles around.

Together with my grandfather—a stickler for organization and tidiness—I was partly responsible for this, and proud of it. Most Saturdays from May until October, I would cut his grass, using a push mower that he kept in the garage. Although gasoline-pow-ered rotary mowers had captured consumers' attention, "Old Betsy" was good enough for him. And I have to admit it worked like a fine Swiss watch, its razor-sharp, whirring steel blades clicking smartly as I walked behind it, its clippings falling tidily into the canvas bag that was attached to its base. Years later, upon marrying and purchasing a home of my own, I would insist with a stubbornness that infuriated my wife on employing push mowers that could be found cheap at garage sales. No matter how much I fussed over these contraptions, however—oiling the wheel assembly and honing the edges of the blades with a grindstone—they never worked as well; they'd snag or cut poorly, and I'd stand there, helpless, cursing my ill fortune. I finally discarded them, one by one, in disgust.

Arriving with my parents and my brothers, Richard and Roger, at my grandfather's stucco, two-story "E-J" house to join my relatives in helping him celebrate his seventy-second birthday, I was reminded yet again of his exalted place as the head of the family. He was showered with more attention than a Hollywood star. A diminutive, demonstrative, fun-loving, prankish man, he basked in the glow of this fame. Consumed by my own sense of self-importance, I was not eager to see someone else—not even my grandfather, who I revered—grab the limelight. I was the eldest of my parents' three boys (a fourth, Randall, would come along as a surprise addition in the fall of 1964). In my own mind at least, I was king of the hill.

I possessed the credentials to support this premise. I was the starting shortstop for a newly organized Babe Ruth-level squad in West Corners; a fixture in the lineup for the managerial brain trust of Gene Brewer, Bob Tingley and Dave Rossi. In two months I would be entering Union-Endicott High School as a sophomore, determined to show the kids from the rough, heavily Italian North Side of Endicott that I was their equal as a "jock;" and, perhaps more importantly, as a Casanova.

None of this mattered that night in my grandfather's yard. The other Lees who pulled their cars alongside the curb in front of his house and who strode forth with salads, casseroles, soft drinks and hamburger and hot dog rolls in tow filled Gram Lee's tiny kitchen and spilled down the back steps into the yard. Their laughter and conversation peppered the warm evening air. The younger children scatted to and fro like chipmunks, being careful to avoid stepping in my grandfather's meticulously maintained flower beds lest they raise the cry of "Get out of there!" from an adult. The men—including my dad, whose name, like my grandfather's, was Horace (Horace Lee Jr.)—and his brothers Bob Lee, Ray Lee and Stewart Lee, all rugged construction men, escaped the heat by congregating on chairs and lounges in my grandfather's screened porch in back. All were present for one reason only: to pay homage to the patriarch.

My grandfather's lawn party resembled the gathering of the Kennedy clan in Hyannisport. It was almost a sin to miss it. It was always circled well in advance on the calendar: a date not to be ignored or underplayed. Neighbors of my grandfather's like Helen Hawthorne, checking out the scene from a yard or more away, or stealing a glance as they walked or drove past, seemed sufficiently impressed. Some would have killed for an invitation. It was a "Lees only" affair, however; admission was granted only to Lees and members of our extended family. Kin came from every direction—and some from distant places—to make an appearance. The festivities lasted for several hours. It was a time to renew the ties that bound us. No gatecrashers were allowed, as the merriment reached a high pitch.

The night was young. The sun had not yet begun to set over my grandfather's house and nearby landmarks: "Round Hill," or "Round Top" (a former Indian stomping ground-turned-lovers' lane); the old iron bridge over the Nanticoke Creek, which connected West Endicott to Glendale; and the Susquehanna River, meandering south from its source, in Cooperstown, toward the Chesapeake Bay. The air was thick with the mesmerizing scent of

marinated lamb, affixed in bite-sized pieces to skewers, being bar-
becued over a charcoal fire: a signal that Uncle Stew was prepar-
ing "spiedies"—an esteemed local dish—for our consumption.
Soon enough, it would be time to eat.

The faces of my smiling loved ones in their short-sleeved blous-
es and open-necked shirts and the specter of my brothers and
younger cousins frolicking on the lawn told me that I belonged
and that all was well. The planets were in precise alignment. The
Lees and the village of Endicott were in exact sync.

It was almost too good to be true.

I would in time learn more about my family's and my village's
colorful histories. My grandfather had been born in Orson,
Pennsylvania in 1888, the fourth of seven children of Charles A.
Lee and Harriet Brown. His father (my great grandfather) was a
farmer and a horse trader. My great grandmother was apparently
part Native American. My grandfather's own reputation as "a
character" predated my relationship with him; I was told that
when he and my grandmother decided to elope, he had boarded a
train at Lakewood, Pennsylvania and signaled her to join him by
pulling the window shade up. Based on the antics I'd become
accustomed to seeing from my grandfather, who relished the
opportunity to entertain visitors with his vaudevillian talents, I
had no difficulty picturing him in this small deceit. I could easily
visualize him, roses in hand, proclaiming to his fellow passengers
on the Erie Railroad that night that he and my grandmother, the
former Lillian B. Stanton, were running off to get married, and
bowing grandly as spontaneous applause erupted around them.

I would also learn, to my surprise, that the thriving community
of Endicott was not as old as I had thought. It had been incorporated just fifty-four years earlier, in 1906. Since that time, it had
sprouted into a modern-day boomtown. E-J's and IBM's factories

and offices stretched along North Street; mercantile activity per-
colated like a coffee pot on Washington Avenue. Lush parks lay
like oases in every nook and cranny of the village.

I resided in the Land of Oz; about that there could be no doubt.

In the euphoria that prevailed that July 3rd over four decades
ago, I had no reason for misgivings. In my sense of well being, in
my excitement over the prospect of finally reaching the halls of
Union-Endicott High School, I was certain that nothing could
rattle my gilded cage. In my bliss, I did not feel the ground shifting underfoot. Everything was as it should be. As if by way of tes-
tament that life could not get any better, word was spreading like
a California wildfire that a U-E grad, Fran Angeline, would be
returning to his alma mater as varsity football coach that very fall.
I could hardly contain my exuberance.

Angeline was a former captain of the Colgate University Red
Raiders, where he had suited up as a "two-way" end under Coach
Hal Lahar. U-E's superintendent, Robert Agone, had wooed
Angeline away from Johnson City High, just up the road.
Delivering Angeline had amounted to a coup d'etat on Agone's
part. Enthusiasm was rampant in Endicott. Most villagers were
sure that Angeline, a detail-oriented and super-charged competitor, would work miracles for the Tigers, who'd managed just a 3-
11-0 record over the previous two seasons. Endicotters were shun-
ning the Tigers as if they were a bunch of lepers. Hopes for a turnaround anytime soon were ebbing. Most of the 50's had been a
bust as far as U-E football was concerned. During a visit I made to
Angeline's house in February of '04, several years after he'd
retired, he recalled a then-member of the U-E faculty, Egbert A.
Thurber, saying to him, by way of discouraging his intentions to
take the U-E coaching position, "why would you want to come
back to this hell hole?"

Faith in the Tigers—once a feared force throughout the "Southern Tier" of New York state, now a doormat—had hit rock bottom. Then came the news that Fran Angeline, a la Superman, was coming to our rescue.

Head-over-heels as we were about sports, my pals and I were aware of Angeline's accomplishments at JC, where, in an unprecedented vote of confidence by that school's administration, he'd been named head coach at the age of twenty-two. We had watched from the bleachers, despondent, as Angeline's Wildcats mudded out a victory over our own legendary-but-past-his-prime coach, Harold V. "Ty" Cobb, in Angeline's rookie year at the helm, in 1957. We knew Angeline had brought a Southern Tier Conference (STC) title to JC the following season.

His credentials were impeccable. Besides, he was one of our own: an Endicotter and a U-E alum.

If anyone could lift our beleaguered Orange and Black out of their doldrums and return pride to "Tiger Town," it was Angeline, who would eventually acquire the nickname "Fran the Man."

As I watched my grandfather, in his ever-present suspenders, blow out the candles on his birthday cake, I did not realize that my tightly stitched universe was coming apart at the seams…that human foibles and festering resentments and jealousies were tearing at the fabric of my family…that my days as a "player" bound for certain athletic stardom were ending as quickly as they'd begun…that I would lose the love of the luscious Laurene Perfetti before she lost her virginity…or that, as if to compound the tragedy, my village—the lustrous shoe town of my birth—was disintegrating. Pompeii, in its day, had fallen. Endicott would fall too.

The physical treasures that had been deposited in our hands like gold nuggets by George F. Johnson were dropping to the wayside, one by one.

The armies of upheaval and destruction were on the march. Before the weekend was over, they would deliver their first, punishing blow.

I never saw them coming.

The then-surviving children of (Grampa) Horace and (Gram) Lillian Lee (from the left): Ray, Horace, Bob, Stew, Harriet, Bessie, Margaret.

The Lee Construction bowling team, 1962-63: Bob Lee; Ray Lee; Dan Lee; Stew Lee; Horace Lee Jr.

West Corners Comes of Age

B y this time, Uncle Stew's incessant drinking had become a source of embarrassment and frustration for the family. My uncle's battle with the bottle introduced a dark cloud to otherwise blue-sky occasions, and gave me one of my first jolts of reality. As I got older I seldom saw my uncle one hundred-percent sober—a disconcerting development, given how I felt about him. Affectionate, gregarious and big-hearted, he was easy to love. I adored him in spite of his weakness.

The seventh-eldest of my grandparents' eleven children, Uncle Stew was, at the age of forty, barreling toward a rendezvous with death just nine years later.

He would become the sixth of seven children my grandmother would lose before her own passing, which didn't come until 1981. Dora, Erwin, Charles Francis and Elizabeth all died in infancy. My Aunt Maggie (Margaret Elizabeth) died in 1963, my Uncle Stew in 1969 and my Aunt Bessie (Bessie May) in 1980.

My grandmother, a frumpy woman—congenial but at the same time stoic and reticent—never spoke of these losses in my presence, but I could tell by instinct and by the references my parents made to them that they lingered on her tongue like a bitter herb. Like the

skin rash on her arms, hands and legs that precipitated bouts of furi-
ous itching (and the scabs to prove it), the deaths of her "little ones"
were a torture that my grandmother shouldered with a gallant
resolve. I would come to compare her steadfastness in the face of
such blows with that of prisoners of war (POWs) who refuse to crack
no matter how sternly their will is tested.

Not even the petunias she loved so much and the pretty white
lace doilies she knitted could lift the burden she carried as The
Woman of Constant Sorrow.

My uncle's death may have been the hardest of all for my grandmother to accept, because of his buoyant personality and squan-
dered promise.

Uncle Stew, like Aunt Maggie, wound up living a significant
portion of his life by my grandparents' side, but for a different reason. Like hers, his was a difficult cross for them to bear.

Poor Aunt Maggie was tormented by demons that would strike
without notice. A thin, bony, hunch-backed, wild-haired woman
with the look of madness in her dark eyes, she suffered from an
epileptic-like condition all the time I knew her. She had been
married briefly. She died seven days after my eighteenth birthday,
in October of 1963. She was only forty-seven years old.

In the evening at my grandfather's house, Aunt Maggie would sit in
a stuffed chair in the corner of the living room, next to the television,
her long fingers playing with the buttons of her plain cotton dress, her
legs (usually unshaven) crossed, her lips twisted in pleasure or pain
(sometimes it was hard to tell which). Often she would be coloring, like
a child. She would press hard with the stub of the crayon she held in
her hand. This exercise would occupy her exertions for hours on end.
She attacked the endeavor with a relentless but dutiful ferocity, taking
great care to stay within the lines as she shadowed in the ears and nose
of a donkey, or the wings of a peacock. She could not speak coherent
words or sentences. Without warning, she would break into laughter,
moan, or let out a squeal that sent shivers up my spine. Often when she
had finished she would look up and, with a quivering arm extended in

my direction, offer the work for my perusal. I considered her colorings to be exemplary objects of art. They were marked by bright hues and a neatness that bordered on precision. She would smile broadly as I nodded my approval, or said in a whisper, "It's good," to her.

Aunt Maggie was a gentle soul except for when she went into one of her "fits."

She scared the daylights out of me.

At fourteen, I was enthralled with Uncle Stew. This stemmed in large part from his natural ebullience, which seemed to float to the surface regardless of the forces aligned against him. I had become accustomed to the smell of liquor on my uncle, and to the telltale cockeyed behavior that marked his personage whenever he was inebriated. My dad and my uncle's other brothers hardly ever touched the stuff; he could not keep his hands off it. And yet his propensity for largess and the obvious affection he felt for those near and dear to him, coupled with a disposition that was invariably buoyant despite the personal predicament in which he might be ensnared at the moment, made him, on balance, an irresistibly lovable man.

So too did his touch with "spiedies." The secret was in the marinade. My uncle's marinade included spearmint leaves. These helped give his spiedies a taste to die for.

Spiedies had apparently developed in the backyards of the hilly North Side of Endicott in the 1920's, if not before. They'd caught fire as a commercial commodity in the mid-1930's when Camilo Iacovelli bought a restaurant on Oak Hill Avenue on the North Side and began making and selling them. Iacovelli went a step farther than anyone else had by combining spiedies on his menu with another coveted local dish—pizza, or "hot pie," which was already an immensely popular entrée at the Cerasaro family's Oaks Inn, a few doors away on the opposite side of Oak Hill Avenue. Buttressed by this pairing of pizza and spiedies, Iacovelli's business skyrocketed.

Throughout the village when I was growing up, legend had it that pizza and spiedies had originated in Endicott, and that talk of them had spread to other parts of the country. All I knew for sure was that no one could match Uncle Stew's spiedies for flavor in West Endicott, at least. His brine with the meat (always lamb) immersed in it sat in the refrigerator for days, gathering potency with each passing minute. Then the meat was extracted from the marinade, threaded onto steel sticks and placed over the open flame. Once charbroiled, it was eaten on Italian bread from Roma's (a bakery in town) or enjoyed straight from the stick—piece by piece. It was usually accompanied by potato salad or a tossed salad.

For his knack with spiedies alone, my uncle was considered to be something of a master chef by all of the Lees.

Uncle Stew was as rowdy an individual as any West Endicott had produced. His outward appearance suggested as much: stubble often adorned his face; tattoos sprang like real vipers from his forearms and shoulders; a yellow tint had seeped like an ink stain into the tips of his fingers (attributable to the many Chesterfields he had smoked over the years). He was full of bombast and brag-gadocio. That he'd accidentally sawed off part of a finger only served to intensify his ruffian nature. His voice, when he wasn't coughing, was as raspy as sandpaper.

His charm, sunny and breezy outlook and huge heart were the reasons I was able to overlook my uncle's shortcomings. I did so until they became too intrusive to ignore.

The weekend following my grandfather's birthday party would reveal to me a side of my uncle that was unnerving to experience, and present to me, although I did not know it then, strong signs that my family, my village and the greater sphere beyond were not the World of Disney incarnations that I had assumed them to be; or that all men were created with the same propensity for upstanding behavior as the mythical and real-life heroes of my youth: the Lone Ranger; Davy Crockett; Robin Hood; Zorro; Roy Rogers; Wyatt Earp. Until then, I had been oblivious to my uncle's imperfections, and to even more troubling situations I was about to encounter. I thought I knew him and my world. I couldn't have been more wrong.

I knew that Uncle Stew and Aunt Honey had tangled like a couple of alley cats, that they'd bounced like pin balls from one dwelling to another, that they left their sons (my cousins Dan and Jack) to fend for themselves for long periods of time and that my uncle was a regular on a bar stool at the Sportsman's Inn. The Sportsman's Inn was a watering hole on Jennings Street in West Endicott. It occupied premises adjacent to my Uncle Bob's mill and only a few blocks from my grandparents' house. It represented as stark a contrast from my grandfather's harmonious haven as could be found. It was a dank, dismal, smelly, noisy nest frequented by hardened alcoholics like my uncle who reveled in one another's often-contentious company.

I also knew that, sober or "smashed," my uncle loved me. The feeling was mutual.

I'd heard stories about my father and my other uncles dragging Uncle Stew home in the middle of the night, rescuing him from his latest drunken brawl or pulling him out of a snow pile before he froze to death. I knew that after consuming a number of beers or shots of whiskey, or both, he'd start popping off at the mouth and that this would sometimes spark an altercation. I'd heard that he'd lead the cops on car chases through the streets of West Endicott, and that he'd spent some nights in the local jail, drying out.

Unlike my Uncle Bob, who was an accomplished boxer as a young man, Uncle Stew was a flop during a brief stab at pugilism. My dad would laugh in relating to me how my uncle "walked right into punches."

— ❖ —

My father and my uncles, proficient carpenters one and all, had figured prominently in the expansion of West Corners during the 1950's. For many years, until about 1929, West Corners—bounded by the Nanticoke Creek to the south and east, the Tioga County line to the west and the hamlet of Union Center to the north—had been an obscure, largely unpopulated community of a few farms and sawmills. Early settlers like Daniel Boswell, Orman West (who operated a farm and sawmill on Day Hollow Road, which is the main thoroughfare) and Orman West's son Martin West and grandson Linneaus W. West were among its more noted inhabitants. As late as 1940, only about 245 families lived in West Corners. Not until L.W. West (for whom the elementary school I attended in the early 1950's is named) began subdividing the family's farm acreage into residential lots did a surge in home building begin. Many of the streets in West Corners that resulted from this carving-up process were named after members of the West family: West; Martin; Leona; Catherine; Grant; Wallace; Carrie; Orman; Irma; and Carl.

These streets became my stomping ground. The first house I remember my parents owning was on Wallace Street, off Day Hollow Road. It was a ranch house my dad had built. In the spring, when the snows melted, a group of us, walking to school, would "race" Popsicle sticks in the tiny, raging streams created along the edges of Wallace Street by the runoff. I cannot say unequivocally that the hollering that myself, my best friend Huey Boyle (who lived directly opposite me) and our fellow contestants directed at these makeshift boats propelled them any more rapidly in the tumbling, muddy water in which they bobbed and weaved, but it turned our otherwise plodding walk down Wallace Street to Day Hollow Road into an adventure. We'd become so engrossed in this frivolity that no one would look up until the troupe reached the Topper Lounge on the other side of Day Hollow Road. The parking lot next to the Topper Lounge provided us with a shortcut to Nanticoke Creek and across the brook to school; when the creek wasn't too high, we'd tiptoe across it on rocks, scramble up the embankment on the other side and scale the chain-link fence behind the school, saving the energy that would have been exerted going all the way to the Day Hollow Restaurant at the end of Day Hollow Road and then north a quarter of a mile or so along Route 26.

Wallace Street was also where I was terrorized by the neighborhood bully "Tonky" Carr, an older boy who lived within sight of my house. The mere specter of this brute standing nearby, like *A Christmas Story*'s despised "Scut" Farkus (Zack Ward), ready to pounce, was enough to send me darting toward my mom's apron strings. In all the years I knew him I never came upon evidence that the friendship between my parents and his (Donald and Crème Carr), who shared good times as members of a small but tight social circle, lessened Tonky's malevolence toward me. My only salvation when he was lurking in the vicinity was my quick feet.

Another West Corners street—steeply inclined Martin Street—was the sledding capital of the neighborhood when I was young. It was on Martin Street, which intersected Hazel Avenue (where my father had built us a new, more comfortable house in the early 1950's) that my brother Roger, disregarding my mother's orders not to ride his bicycle there because of the street's treacherous pitch, took a header and fell to the ground, unconscious. My brother Richard, who'd witnessed the accident, was overcome by dread as he brought news of the calamity to my mother. "Mom, come quick," Richard, breathless as he burst into the house, said. "I think Roger's dead!" "Let's go," my mother said, heading toward the car. "I'm not going back *there*!" Rich responded.

In the 1950's, the sounds of the Lee men's hammers and power saws reverberated throughout West Corners as new houses went up in every part of the community. My dad—who was called "Junior" or "Junie," not Horace, most of the time—was a top-notch framing carpenter, as were my Uncle Stew and my Uncle Ray. They attrib-

uted this in part to starting their day with coffee and doughnuts at
Matt Makowski's restaurant: Yum Yum Corner. Nothing interfered
with this ritualistic gathering of tradesmen, which included not only
my dad and my uncles but also electricians and plumbers and
masons and plasterers they worked with or knew. At the Yum
Yum—which sat at the intersection of Day Hollow Road and Rt. 26,
kitty corner from the Day Hollow Restaurant—my father, his brothers and my dad's pal Bud Bogart would place their orders and begin
bantering, teasing and arguing good-naturedly before heading to the
job site. No one was immune from the barbs tossed back and forth,
even the Yum Yum's owner, the crew cut and always-affable Matt
Makowski, who willingly engaged in the repartee even while scrambling eggs and buttering toast. Makowski gave as good as he got
when it came to exchanging digs.

In the late summer of 1960 at the Yum Yum, conjecture flowed
hard and fast about whether U-E's football team—with Fran
Angeline about to take charge—would devour, or be eaten alive,
by the Ithaca's and Binghamton North's of the venerable old
"STC" (Southern Tier Conference).

It was against this backdrop of convivial daily trips to the Yum Yum
and on to a nearby house project during the summer months that my
cousin Jack and I, who were close in age, received our indoctrination
as apprentice carpenters. It was a hard education. The sheepishness
we felt as greenhorns being singled out for innocuous scorn (or, more
rarely, for effusive praise) by our elders while sipping coffee at the Yum
Yum represented a perturbing challenge, the implications of which
manifested themselves in the sudden redness that colored our cheeks.
More difficult still was the derision to which we were subjected as we
struggled to learn the mechanics of the ancient craft of carpentry.
Whether it was trying to drive spikes, laying down a chalk line, cutting treads for stairs, raising partitions or hauling shingles up a ladder,
Jack and I didn't seem to have the aptitude for the assignment. These
inadequacies delighted our instructors, who hooted their disapproval
of our technique even while exhibiting the patience of saints. We

were especially inept on a scaffold. More than once, after tumbling ingloriously from the rickety platform our mentors had built so that they could plywood the outside of a house, apply siding or get to the roof, Jack and I—our bones intact but our egos shattered—would look up from the drainage ditch surrounding the foundation to see three faces smirking down at us.

His shortcomings on a scaffold notwithstanding, Jack, who was wily and wiry, went on to become a standout lightweight wrestler at U-E High School for Coach Frank "Sarge" Sorochinsky.

By the time the Summer of 1960 rolled around my dad and his brothers had helped construct more than fifty houses in a new subdivision my Uncle Bob's Lee Window Unit Co. had put up in a pocket of West Corners called Neal Heights, on Neal Road, in the Morlando Drive area off Day Hollow Road. They had also done the grunt work for my Uncle Bob in building several more houses on a new street he'd opened just north of Neal Road.

Meanwhile my Uncle Bun—Bernard Turner, who'd married my Aunt Harriet—ran a construction company that equaled my Uncle Bob's in its ability to erect houses at a frenetic pace. Both men had acquired a degree of wealth and comfort from their endeavors. Among the houses my Uncle Bun built during the construction boom that took place in West Corners were ones on Crestview Drive, not far from Hazel Avenue, that were occupied by friends of my parents: the Mitchells; the Titmans; and others. These couples were regulars on Friday and Saturday nights at our house, where card playing, particularly involving the game of Canasta, took place until well past dark. They came around too for Saturday-night dance parties in our finished basement.

Although my Uncle Bob and Uncle Bun were both of below-average height, they shared an iron will. For a brief time all of the adult men in my life—my dad, my uncles Bob, Ray, Stew and Bun and my cousin Dan (Jack's older brother)—bowled together at Roy Rosencrance's Ideal Lanes in West Endicott. What Uncle Bob and Uncle Bun lacked in the skills required for proficiency in bowling they made up for with a determination that knew no limit. Both refused to accept a tally of 150 when 200 was attainable, and they used whatever resources they could muster to get the job done even if they didn't look especially stylish doing it. In his own zeal to post a high number, Uncle Bun did not bother himself with the sweet sciences of technique; he simply charged toward the lane and rocketed the sixteen-pound ball forward with a mighty windmill motion, convinced that the results were directly proportional to the speed at which the projectile was moving. The laminated wooden sticks, nestled in the shape of a rack of balls on a pool table, must have shared his sentiment on this matter, because they often fell accommodatingly, possibly out of sheer trepidation.

My Uncle Ray was a pretty fair country bowler, laying the ball down with a whisper and going straight at the "1-2" pocket from the port side. My dad, also a lefty, took a lot of ribbing for his habit of dropping the ball like a ton of bricks from his hip, so that it landed with a thud before beginning its roll down the alley.

Bowling was a pursuit that brought the men of the family together in a shared purpose. It allowed them to forget their differences. It also eventually produced newspaper headlines, trophies and respect; my brothers Richard and Roger later demonstrated in abundance as virtual semi-professionals many of the skills their elders lacked. As of February of 2003, my southpaw-slinging brother Roger had recorded eight perfect 300 games—earning himself induction into the Endicott Bowling Association (EBA) Hall of Fame.

West Corners was emerging as a place to be reckoned with. From my perspective the neighborhood, though still a poor second cousin to Endicott, measured up handsomely. I was earning good money from a paper route, delivering the *Binghamton Press* to homes in and around Day Hollow Road (while being careful to avoid the vicious German shepherd "King," who lurked behind one of my customer's homes). I had the run of the roost. On a hot day I could drop by the Day Hollow Restaurant or the Topper Lounge for a complimentary glass of water to quench my thirst. Any time the spirit moved me when I was out and about I could open the screen door of Duffy's (a store on Day Hollow Road) to buy some penny candy or baseball cards, visit Burton Franklin's Cities Service station on Route 26 or Anthony Innone's West Corners Garage on Carl Street to put air in my bicycle's tires, drift toward Dr. Giordano's house on Glendale Drive (opposite Bosket Pond) to see if my friend Tom Giordano was around, or stop at Sam Sergi's barber shop on the side of the Day Hollow Restaurant for a haircut.

Despite all of this, my life was not without concerns. At home, my parents would discuss the problems Uncle Stew's drinking was causing. At the Yum Yum and during breaks on the job, I'd hear complaints about my Uncle Bob's lack of appreciation for the contributions my dad and his brothers had made to the success of Lee Window. Lee Window was getting bigger and sassier by the minute, but they were restless. His dissatisfaction finally led my Uncle Ray to leave my Uncle Bob's employ and establish his own construction company.

My seemingly unblemished family was showing signs of fray. So too was my village: soon enough, Endicott would lose Endicott-Johnson. With the loss of E-J would come the demise of Washington Avenue: "The Avenue."

Endicott would never be the same.

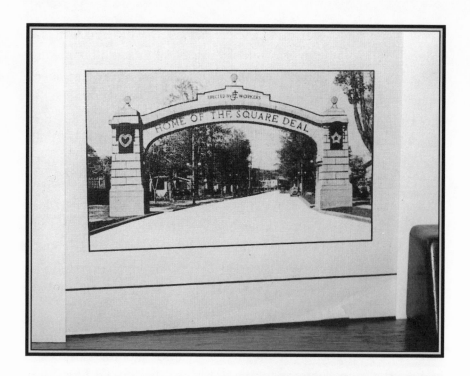

Above: The "Home of the Square Deal" arch; a still-standing symbol of "the E-J years" in Endicott, it was erected by E-J workers as a tribute to company co-founder George F. Johnson, and dedicated on Labor Day, 1920.

To right: George F. Johnson in Florida, where he wintered.

AN ARCH FOR "GEORGE F."

E ndicott, before its demise, was almost too good to believe. In keeping with the image of masculine aloofness expected of me by my male friends, I feigned indifference to this fact. Although I seldom outwardly acknowledged it, I understood that the village had been blessed in many ways. Adults gave a single person credit for this phenomenon: George F. Johnson.

Johnson had died in 1948, the year I turned three. Photos I'd seen of him when he was young depicted a lanky man with small shoulders, a long, straight nose and friendly eyes. They also revealed that he favored three-piece suits. Everything we owned or enjoyed, it appeared, came from him. Johnson was typical of the founders of great institutions who, as Emerson noted, continue to "cast a long shadow" even after they are gone.

In some ways Johnson reminded me of the anonymous benefactor of a thirty-minute television show, "The Millionaire," that was popular for about five years starting in the mid-50's. With each new episode of the program, the reclusive manufacturer and multimillionaire John Beresford Tipton (whose voice was portrayed by Paul Frees) would send an emissary—Michael Anthony (played by Marvin Miller)—to unsuspecting individuals' doors to present them with a tax-free cashier's check for one million dollars. The only condition attached to the transaction was that the recipients of the money must never divulge how they had acquired their fortune.

"The Millionaire" made for terrific theater. Viewers tuned in each week to see whether those who got the windfall used the dollars wisely, or imprudently.

Like "The Millionaire," Johnson seemed to draw satisfaction from helping people get ahead; in his case, it was his workers and their families and, by extension, the village at large. His humanitarian tendencies surfaced in unusual and endearing ways. Johnson insisted, for instance, that E-J parking lots be open to all, not just to his own employees. This practice contrasted sharply with the one adopted by his counterparts at IBM, whose parking lots—in part because of the sensitive nature of some of the company's work for the government—were monitored by security personnel and surrounded by chain-link fence.

Johnson went to extraordinary lengths to ensure the health and happiness of the E-J family and the community. There did not appear to be anything self-serving about his acts of kindness. Convinced, for instance, that the game of golf was second only to playgrounds in its capacity to refresh the spirit, he had a links built for his workers. He selected flat, relatively undemanding terrain near the river in West Endicott for this club, called En-Joie, so that golfers, stressed from a day or week's work in the factory, could walk the fairways easily and quickly. The greens fee to play the course remained a quarter for as long as E-J owned the property (which it subsequently sold to the village), and it was a public course in every sense of the word; all were welcome.

It was while lifting short-iron shots onto a fairway from his front yard on Swartwood Avenue, abutting the course, that a golfing prodigy, Richie Karl, whose father worked for E-J, first caught the public's attention. Karl flashed onto the scene like a meteor; over the span of two decades, culminating in a sudden-death playoff victory over a seasoned veteran, Australian Bruce Crampton, in the B.C. Open in 1974, the rail-thin but powerful Karl, whose drives left his clubs as if launched from a cannon, won everything in sight around upstate New York. At the height of what appeared to be certain long-term stardom as the new golden boy of the PGA Tour, with the bold swagger of a young Arnold Palmer in his hips, he disappeared as quickly as he'd arrived. Until he drifted off to Iowa, seldom to be seen or heard from again, Richie Karl had authored a storybook tale that caused the chest of every Endicotter, young and old, to swell with pride. He was the latest in a string of notables the village had produced: the magnetic Johnny "Yachta" Logan, who had become the starting shortstop for the Milwaukee Braves; Ron "Loosh" Luciano, who'd achieved national raves as a lineman at Syracuse University and then gone on to play professional football and to become a major league baseball umpire with a flair for showboating that the game had seldom seen; and Johnny Hart, the award-winning syndicated cartoonist.

Richie Karl had risen to the top faster than any of the others; while Hart's "B.C." first appeared in print in newspapers on the eve of his twenty-seventh birthday, Karl had begun making headlines as a mere schoolboy.

That Richie Karl had pulled off his first and only PGA Tour triumph on his home turf, at En-Joie, before thousands of adoring hometown fans, in an event bearing the same name as Johnny Hart's comic strip, made the afternoon of his breakthrough win all that more exquisite.

George F. Johnson's name was not mentioned in the evening glow of the trophy presentation on the 18th green at En-Joie that Sunday in 1974. But in creating En-Joie in the first place, Johnson had set the stage even for the arrival of Richie Karl years later. And for the emergence of Alex Alexander, the impetuous and ambitious son of an early Union restaurateur, who became synonymous with the growth of the B.C. Open as the tournament's chairman.

— ❖ —

The same good instincts that led to the creation of En-Joie also inspired Johnson to lay the groundwork for Endicott's first full-service hospital, so that E-J'ers did not have to travel several miles east, to Johnson City or Binghamton, for medical care. Johnson donated the land and one hundred fifty thousand dollars towards construction of the four-story building, and used a local architect and local doctors to develop plans for the facility. Built on Round Hill, with a picturesque view of the Susquehanna River looking east from its perch, Ideal Hospital was completed in two years. It opened in 1927. Doctors were thrilled with its cheery atmosphere; patients and visitors appreciated its many splendid features, especially its 18,000 square foot sun porch.

Like E-J's parking lots and En-Joie Golf Club, the hospital was for the use of all.

In 1929, a Nurses Home, next door, opened; this building was made possible by money given by George F. Johnson's wife, in memory of her sister.

En-Joie Golf Club and Ideal Hospital illustrated conclusively that there was no limit to the Johnson family's eagerness to be a loving steward of the village it called home.

By the summer of 1960, I was well aware that I had been born at Ideal Hospital (in October of 1945), that I had almost bled to death having my tonsils removed there at a young age, and that it was the place Endicotters turned to when they needed emergency treatment, surgery or other attention related to their physical health. I did not learn until much later that the construction of the hospital was another in a long line of good deeds Johnson had done for Endicott. Or that he'd actually begun the initiative back in 1917 by having a small infirmary set up in E-J's Sole Leather Tannery, and that this operation had quickly grown to involve six doctors and six nurses, and that its rapid evolution had led to the start-up of an emergency hospital on Odell Avenue in Endicott for the care of E-J workers from the North Side and then to the launch of a site on Washington Avenue (E-J Medical) for maternity care and minor surgical procedures.

E-J Medical moved from Washington Avenue into new quarters on North Street around 1940 and was a busy place, frequented by, among many others, my grandparents, for an assortment of needs.

My grandparents lived in an "E-J house," common throughout Endicott and West Endicott. These houses were small but functional, usually consisting of a basement, one entrance in front, one on the side and one to the rear, a front porch (theirs was enclosed), a living room, dining room and kitchen on the first floor and two or three bedrooms and a bathroom upstairs. At fourteen, their house seemed like a dollhouse to me, it was so undaunting. Loping three steps at a time, I could bound up the stairs to the bathroom in a few seconds; when my dad and his brothers and their wives and the children gathered in the living room to watch Gillette's Cavalcade of Sports (the "Friday Night Fights") on television, it was literally standing room only.

As with the gigantic pool at En-Joie Park in which I learned to swim and the hospital in which I first drew breath, these homes were a George F. Johnson exclusive. Although my grandparents' house was not nearly as spectacular as non-E-J homes like the showcase ones my Uncle Bob built for himself and others, or as roomy as ranch houses my dad and my Uncle Ray and Uncle Bun constructed in West Corners and elsewhere, it had its redeeming qualities, not the least of which was its intimacy. Also, my grandfather kept a basket of butternuts at the bottom of the basement stairs!

My grandparents had previously owned one of the first E-J homes built, on South Street in Union near the banks of the river. My dad spent the first few years of his life there, before the family moved to West Endicott. E-J homes were initially built just on the south side of town. Curiously, the conditions allowing for their construction initially contained deed-restriction language that made them available only to people of Anglo-Saxon and Irish origin; throughout the 1920's and beyond, they began popping up like jack-in-the-boxes: on the streets of the North Side and in West Endicott and eventually even to the newer neighborhood of West Corners. Italians, Slavs, Russians and Poles joined the many immigrants from European countries who eventually acquired E-J homes.

The arrangement that made this possible reflected still another redeeming side of George F. Johnson's character. The occupants of the houses purchased their homes for a sum of about three thousand dollars, and paid for them by payroll deduction in the amount of approximately seven dollars a week with an interest rate of one to five percent attached. Johnson sweetened the deal by incorporating into the purchase agreement the provision that the weekly payment could be "reclaimed" by the buyer if requested; in typical "George F." style, he also made paint and other upkeep materials available to homeowners free of charge so that they could take pride in the maintenance of their residences. It begs credulity to imagine any of today's profit-conscious corporations extending such an opportunity to their employees!

Prior to their retirement, both of my grandparents worked for E-J; they and other members of my family spoke fondly of George F. Johnson. Johnson's influences on life in Endicott were so numerous that it is difficult today, as it was 1960, to name one impact he made that was of greater significance than another. E-J homes would certainly be high on the list. The free pair of shoes he gave to all schoolchildren at Christmas time would be too. Several choices of shoes were offered; the boys preferred the "hi-cuts" because those came with a pocket in one of them. Inside the pocket was a jackknife.

In my mind, cluttered with thoughts of sports gods like Mickey Mantle of the New York Yankees, Bob Pettit of the St. Louis Hawks, Oscar Robertson of the Cincinnati Royals and Alan Ameche and Johnny Unitas of the Baltimore Colts, I allowed room for only the inkling of recognition that our village was an extraordinary place. The evidence of this was hard to ignore, nevertheless. There were the parks. Premier among these was En-Joie Park, the village's shimmering lady. There was West Endicott Park, a few blocks from my grandparents' house. There was Mersereau Park, where I learned to play baseball—and where I was selected to suit up for the Little League team sponsored by Marine Midland Bank. There was North Side Park. Everywhere one turned, there was a park.

The arch that straddled Main Street a short distance west of the high school—the "E-J Workers Arch," under which motorists passed heading west toward Vestal, Union, West Endicott, Campville or Owego, or east toward Endwell, Johnson City or Binghamton—was to Endicott what the Eiffel Tower was to Paris, Big Ben was to London or the Brooklyn Bridge was to New York City. My interest in how the arch came to exist would not surface until later in life. At fourteen, it fascinated me strictly as an architectural wonder. Eventually I would learn that E-J workers had come up with the fourteen thousand dollars necessary to erect the structure, that it was built of solid blocks of litholite, that its enormous bases each measured six feet by eight feet, that bronze tablets with a bust of the workers' illustrious employer on them adorned the right supporting columns from either direction and that the arch had been dedicated on "George F. Day" in September of 1920. In my admittedly limited travels I had seen nothing to compare with it; it was a piece de resistance. The arch provoked in me a feeling of awe mixed with wariness. Its bases abutted the road, which curved slightly at that spot; whenever the family sedan approached the arch's space, the sensation one experienced from the back seat, as the vehicle hurtled forward, was that there was no way to get past the abutments without ending up as a pile of rubble in the middle of the road. So I would cover my eyes and hope for the best. Fortunately, catastrophe of the sort I'd imagined never befell us.

Amazingly, the arch still stands today despite repeated and often near-successful attempts to remove it, and has in fact been refortified. It is one of the few artifacts from E-J's glory days that have survived. Many of the others disappeared from the village's landscape one by one, snatched away like abducted children when villagers weren't looking, leaving in the wake of their awful vanishing act a community sadly lacking many of the telltale evidences that E-J, and George F. Johnson, had once been a presence at all.

The knowledge of E-J's, and Endicott's, grandeur is of little comfort today to those who felt it first-hand...their hearts yearn with a temptation to crawl into a time capsule and take a voyage back to an era when the village possessed the qualities they remember so well. If only George F. Johnson himself could be reincarnated, to start anew the grand design...

From the instant George F. Johnson and Henry B. Endicott helped found Endicott in the early 1900's until E-J's factories and tanneries began closing their doors in 1968, by which time the village had begun its slide into virtual extinction, Johnson's commitment to the community never wavered. His impact spread to every corner of the village, providing old and young alike with a life they could not have dreamed was possible.

Uncle Stew seemed even more oblivious to these endowments than me. The pristine homes and parks and playgrounds, The Avenue, even the expectation of the revival of U-E football fortunes under Fran Angeline—the prodigal son returned—did not appear to have any visible effect on my uncle. He was drinking heavier than ever...at the Sportsman's Inn, at home and elsewhere. He was about to jar me out of the cushy cubby hole in which I was nestled and to provide me with one of the first lessons I would receive that life is full of reversals and hard knocks.

Things couldn't have been better, and then they took a turn for the worse.

The author's Grade 3 class at West Corners Elementary School, 1954.
(I am the second student back in the second row from the right).

Our "Field of Dreams"

Between the three-bedroom house atop a hill in West Corners that my father had built for us in 1953 and the seemingly ideal circumstances in which I found myself immersed every day, my world was practically without flaw in July of 1960. Like Goldilocks cavorting in the den of the three bears and fortified by the bowl of porridge she had prepared for herself, I harbored no suspicions as regards the difficulties that were about to drop like a sledgehammer onto my youthful brow.

As soon as my father mounted a backboard and iron rim over the garage door, our driveway became a microcosm of Madison Square Garden; on any given day, the neighborhood would gather for games of H-O-R-S-E, "Around the World," "21," or two-on-two or three-on-three. My infatuation with sports was so intense that in the dead of winter long after nightfall the methodical pitter-patter of the ball would continue, even if I occupied the court alone—persevering with fingers gone numb from the wet and cold. All it took was the illumination cast from a desk lamp that I propped in the living room's small side window, next to the driveway.

Sometimes my father, short and stocky, would bow to my insistent demands and shoot hoop with me. He possessed the deadliest two-handed set shot I had ever seen until I arrived at U-E High School and witnessed Bob Wurtenburg, the school's varsity basketball coach and later its athletic director, dazzle onlookers by dropping one set shot after another from near mid-court with an effortless flick of his wrists. "Wurt" was a tall man with closely-cropped hair, big ears, big hands and a warm personality. I took an instant liking to him.

During tryouts for the varsity basketball team my junior year, after recovering from a knee injury, I impressed Wurt with my ability to dribble and shoot, but he still lopped me from the squad in the final round of cuts. "I need someone tall," he said, explaining why he chose Rodney Moore, a gangling classmate, instead of me. My ears burned in indignation, but I couldn't bring myself to hate Wurt. I still attended every game and rooted vociferously for the Tigers, even as I wished I was on the floor with Fred Karaman, Bobby Atkinson, Mike Nalevanko, Tommy Giordano and the rest of the squad Bob Wurtenburg had selected.

Wurt seemed pleased when, years later, I became a sportswriter. He always went out of his way to make sure I was comfortable as I settled into my seat in the press box at Ty Cobb Stadium at the start of a football game, and received me with a cordial air whenever I dropped by his office near the new gym in a new wing of the building to get the latest scoop on Tiger athletics.

I don't think my father had my individual happiness in mind when he chose the lot on Hazel Avenue in the then-developing area of West Corners for our home, but he could not have picked a location that was more ideally suited to the fancies of a kid like me—enamored as I was with any activity involving the outdoors. My long side yard became a football field in the fall and a baseball diamond in the spring. It was the place where I first watched the runt-sized but sinewy Mike Stone boom punts high into the air and deep downfield, and where it first became apparent to me that big Al Rossi's knees could rattle a would-be tackler's teeth loose from their moorings. On the slow, steamy, lazy days of summer the shallow yard behind my house was turned into a whiffle-ball diamond, complete with limed baselines. The large plate-glass dining-room window sat squarely in the line of fire from the batter's box. My mother would jump out of her skin as white plastic spheroids ricocheted off the green-stucco back wall of the house, or against the windows over the kitchen sink or the oft-violated dining-room window. How that window stood up to the repeated drubbings it received is still a mystery to me, but at the time it was of little concern. The preoccupation of the whiffle-ball players was with who would "lead the league" in extra-base hits, and we kept careful track of these statistics. "Off the house" was a double, "onto the roof" a triple, "over the roof" into the front yard a home run.

We bashed whiffle balls as if there was no tomorrow. As they began to break from the repeated drubbings and then to fall apart entirely, we patched them up with electrical tape. When they finally died for good, we bought more of them from Fred Zappia's sporting-goods store on The Avenue.

The covered patio that served as our front porch was where we gathered in our idle moments. It was also where we listened to broadcasts of the Yankee games on the radio while devouring the pizza from Felix Roma's bakery that my mother brought home every Friday night. We washed the pizza down with Coca-Cola, Pepsi-Cola or Hires Root Beer, bottles of which sat on the kitchen counter. The pizza arrived in huge sheets and was cut up into squares; my brothers and I and our friends took comfort in the fact that the pizza was close at hand, and that it would provide instantaneous relief all weekend when our stomachs began to growl or when fatigue or boredom set in. Meals on the fly were common for the pack of urchins with which I ran, usurped as were our energies with the diversions to which boys our age were drawn. There was lots of exploring to do, and we set out like Meriwether Lewis and William Clark in an effort to climb the weedy hill behind Chuck Mitchell's house on Crestview Drive that led to a clearing at the base of the utility pole at the top of the incline, to re-visit time and again a small waterfall and other places hidden deep in the woods and to walk the rocky edges of Nanticoke Creek east from an access point along Day Hollow Road until we reached the narrow two-lane bridge: West Corners' most-direct link with West Endicott.

The old bridge became our hideout. By scrambling up the banks above the creek we could climb into the circular portals that hung like rings below the bridge, and from the obscurity of that sanctuary, with the sounds of the creek's waters, underneath, and the road's traffic, overhead, ringing in our ears, engage in every manner of mischievous pursuit. Smoking, though high on our list of preoccupations during these moments of clandestine foolishness, was by no means the most favored. That distinction went to perusing baseball card-sized black and white pictures of men and women in various stages of undress or sexual intercourse that we'd obtained from an older acquaintance, or studying photos of naked vixens that had been torn from the pages of a girlie magazine.

In time Roma's pizza gave way to Nirchi's pizza in the taste war at the Lee house. Isn't that always the way? The things we consider to be indispensable ingredients in our lives, those items that are thought to be so inherently good in every respect that they become seemingly irreplaceable, are ultimately (and all too soon) upstaged by another, better product, or they simply cease to exist altogether. Growing up, Roma's pizza commanded attention and respect even though, like a Ford, it was a relatively uncomplicated commodity, consisting of a plain but thick breaded base, a firm crust and a solid layer of tomato sauce dashed with a sprinkling of cheese. Roma's was our family's first choice for pizza for years. It was also available over the counter virtually everywhere in the village, and was a hot seller at the concession stand at Ty Cobb Stadium as fans waited for the Tigers to surge forth from their locker room in the wooden clubhouse at the eastern end of the field. Then we discovered Nirchi's pizza, a Cadillac by comparison. Suddenly a rival with a more savory taste had emerged. Our allegiances switched. From the cramped ground-level bakery on the North Side of Endicott from which Nirchi's operated, pizza pies fluttered out the door like birds taking flight.

Similarly, the old bridge with its sanctuaries—the best place for forbidden delights I'd ever known—was eventually supplanted by a new road and new bridge into West Corners that followed the westerly edge of Nanticoke Creek (instead of the eastern banks). With the creation of this more-direct entryway into my neighborhood came the elimination of the old concrete bridge—a bridge that had had a purpose much different from the one our parents believed to be its sole function. Gone, but not forgotten. During the years that the old bridge existed, no adult ever set foot in our private refuge; shadowed chambers that, though open to the light on either end, nevertheless afforded a spot to congregate that was out of reach of all those except the most nimble (and daring) climbers. During the period that the old bridge stood, no one over the age of seventeen participated in the sordid childhood shenanigans that transpired so close to the constant flow of humanity back and forth, and yet so far. This was our den of inequity. Here, experimentation of such a ribald nature occurred that we would have been ashamed to share the embarrassing details with respectable older folks. So we kept quiet about it.

The disappearance of the old bridge and our abandonment of Roma's in favor of a tastier competitor were a ways off. Of more immediate import was the upcoming Saturday-afternoon baseball game between West Corners and Endwell on the new ball field behind the West Corners Elementary School that those of us from West Corners had scratched into being with our bare hands. Whipped to a frenzy of fervor for the task by our manager and coaches—Gene Brewer, Bob Tingley and Dave Rossi—and drawing inspiration from Mr. Brewer, whose strapping physique suggested that hard labor was not a hindrance that would deter us for long, and compelled further by an eagerness to have a field of our own, we raked and hoed and mowed and carted rocks off by the wheel-barrow-full in searing heat for days on end. We worked like a chain gang. We unloaded the rocks in a pile beyond the outfield. When the job was done, we threw a snow fence around the outer perimeter. Slowly and painfully a baseball diamond had taken shape out of a barren piece of land, complete with a dirt infield, a pitcher's mound, home and away benches and foul poles in left and right field. Much of West Corners had materialized and was in fact still coming together in the short time since my family had taken up residence on Hazel Avenue. My father and my uncles had built many of the new homes in our neighborhood and along Day Hollow Road and in the area of Morlando Drive. Now, as if to reinforce the notion that West Corners, a little finger on the big hand of the Union-Endicott school district, was coming of age, there was a ball field to brag about. And it was ours.

Game time was only a few hours away. Concerns filled my head. Would I bat third, or eighth, in the lineup? Would Dave Brewer, our best pitcher, have his good breaking ball? Would Kevin Cahill, our sure-gloved third baseman, be on top of his game? I couldn't wait to put on my flannels with the words *West Corners* emblazoned across the front, and to don my hose, cap and black steel spikes.

My parents would be among those in attendance. They were faithful spectators in their lawn chairs, cheering ardently and without let-up from behind the backstop. "Perfetti" would be there too. I couldn't wait to show off for her. Afterwards there would be the short ride to Vivona's root-beer stand for root beer floats.

As I oiled down my glove and bounced a tennis ball off the front steps to loosen up, everyone was making plans to take in the game.

Including Uncle Stew.

Three classmates (left to right): Jeanne Randesi, Bob Atkinson and Roslyn D'Amado.

A Rude Awakening

W e had crafted a stony field of dreams, and bore the blisters on our hands and the aches in our backs to prove it. We had sacrificed mightily in our attempt to provide West Corners with an asset comparable to the touted ball field on Page Avenue in West Endicott, or the one at North Side Park in Endicott. Upon the rough-hewn West Corners diamond, and elsewhere, I was to absorb, over the course of several summers and in seemingly equal proportion, highs and lows of the sort that in time I came to conclude are an inescapable part of one's journey through life. These, for good or ill, I received at the feet of the people who the Maker, in His wisdom (or in His moments of indiscretion), had determined should be my companions along the way.

I was under no illusion that any astute observer would rank our new field in West Corners on a level with Page Avenue. Page Avenue I considered third in stature only to the big ball yard in the Bronx that the New York Yankees called home and the one in Johnson City (Johnson Field) on which the Binghamton Triplets, a farm team of the New York Yankees, played. These other premier fields had age itself going for them; as a result, loose pebbles like the ones that would tear our flesh when we attempted to slide into second or third base, or home plate, had, in Page Avenue's case, for instance, been raked loose and removed, so as to pose no hindrance to life or limb. The keepers of these other diamonds had attained such a degree of familiarity with their fields that the task of grooming them had become a relatively manageable, it not entirely predictable, proposition. Their fields were clipped and cropped neat as a pin, like the heads of men who frequented Sam Sergi's barbershop in West Corners, or Howard Yeager's in Endicott.

Page Avenue, a short walk from West Endicott Park (one had to cross the tracks of the Erie Railroad, striding in a southerly direction for a block or so, past the E-J factory, on the right, and Fusco's restaurant, on the left, to reach it), was to me a sacred plot, on which only ballplayers of inestimable ability were allowed to set foot. I liked the cut of it; it was tucked onto a corner lot at the intersection of Page Avenue and Marion Street, and was bounded, to its immediate rear, by the elevated, gleaming tracks on which the Erie Railroad's trains steamed past and, at the opposite end, beyond the outfield (which was unfenced) by Marion Street in left and centerfield, and Page Avenue in right center and right. Across Marion Street sat a row of houses, the yards of which were within reach of those husky batsmen who could regularly, or even occasionally, take a pitch high and deep. How many serene evenings sipping a drink on their front porches were interrupted by the thump of a baseball hopping across the lawn or banging against the stoop for the residents of these homes, I cannot say; too many, were they themselves to render a number for consideration, I am sure.

Of Page Avenue's many attributes, not the least of which were enclosed dugouts for the home and away teams, wooden bleachers, an enormous backstop and a press box, I viewed as its finest by far the set of lights attached to tall wooden poles that surrounded the field. These, when lit, cast a mesmerizing glow. To me, Page Avenue was the Mercedes Benz of local fields, especially in the evening when, driving by with my parents, it glistened like a gem in the black of night. I dreamed incessantly about Page Avenue, musing as I lay on my back on my bed, whether a kid from West Corners would ever get to romp with the boys and men from West Endicott who played baseball and softball there. The opportunity came sooner than I thought. One afternoon at summer playground, the boys were rustled together, told to gather their gear and to pile into a couple of taxicabs for the ride to West Endicott Park. To our usual lineup of friendly competition between the opposing summer playground teams—box hockey and badminton—that brought West Corners to West Endicott, and vice versa, had been added, this day, a baseball game at Page Avenue. The excited beating of the hearts of those lucky enough to be selected to undertake this mission would have been sufficient to propel our vehicles successfully to their destination, had their gasoline tanks come up empty en route.

With strikeouts on three trips to the plate that day against a West Endicott pitcher whose speedballs, as Bruce Springsteen would say, "could make you look like a fool, boy," and a dumb error at shortstop to boot, I was accorded an early warning that my own "Glory Days" might be short-lived. And that the careers of other ballplayers, like West Endicott's lefty-swinging clean-up hitter, Carl Letson, who I was seeing in action for the first time, might be just starting to take off. It was one of the first lessons I would receive in the difference between being a "phenom" on a small stage and just another run-of-the-mill player when cast amid the big boys.

The next few years would bring euphoria mixed with heartache. Fizzling out as an athlete after demonstrating such promise during my early boyhood was a hard development to accept. There would be others.

The friendship that developed between Carl Letson and I would be put to the test in our years at U-E, where, emboldened by a confidence in his athletic abilities that was unshakable, Carl emerged as a wunderkind in his chosen game while I drifted into the shadows reserved for those whose role it is to merely watch. All too soon I found myself to be just another fan at U-E games, cheering vociferously for Carl to deliver one of the blistering line drives down the right-field line for which he'd become celebrated and to cement his reputation as a feared hitter in Maurice "Hammy" Hamilton's lineup even as I cursed the bedevilments that prevented me from realizing similar acclaim. The visions I'd harbored of becoming "another Johnny Logan," just as Endicott's immortal "Yachta" had propelled himself in a fantastic leap from the playing fields of Endicott to the starting lineup of the Milwaukee Braves, were in short order to be dashed...smashed to bits on a rocky coast.

I'd heard stories about Johnny Logan's days at U-E, including descriptions of how, more than once, he'd crushed baseballs into the river behind the school, a prolific blast; these exploits I put in a class with Mickey Mantle's five hundred-foot homers, even as I wondered if the tales about Logan's legendary feats were true. One thing was already apparent to me: as a "good-field, no-hit" player, I wasn't on the verge of becoming another Johnny Logan. A bum knee, courtesy of my days as a member of the freshman basketball team at Jennie F. Snapp, was threatening to turn me from a neighborhood superstar to a high school has-been. My visits to a doctor on Washington Avenue who drained fluid from my left knee once a week for months on end were pure agony; I soon decided that the physical discomfort involved in this procedure was not nearly so demoralizing, however, as the awareness that my capacity to run and jump was being compromised. And that I might never again do either quite as well.

It was with these first seeds of doubt about my long-term prospects as a jock creeping into mind that I prepared for West Corners' clash with Endwell. As I engaged in a game of "pepper" with Bobby Muir and Tom Morris along the first-base line, an unmistakable sense of excitement enveloped our bench. A new game for West Corners' new "nine" was at hand.

A suspicion that something was wrong nagged at me too, however.

Behind our bench, Uncle Stew had taken a spot next to my parents, eager to root his son (my cousin Jack) and myself and our teammates on to victory.

"Attaboy, Rod. . .give 'em hell," he hollered as I came to the plate for the first time. His voice could be heard above all the others, and was lathered with the inflection of someone who'd been drinking. The back of my neck flushed.

I went down on three pitches and trudged back to the bench. The sight of his nephew fanning so futilely at the plate did nothing to diminish my uncle's giddy attitude.

"You'll get them next time, Rod," he shouted. "That ragarm ain't got diddly," he added, pointing a finger toward the opposing pitcher. I squirmed self-consciously, pawing at the dirt with my cleats.

My uncle had decided to get an early start on a weekend of letting loose. He had more surprises in store for us, as I was soon to find out.

Switch-hitting Mickey Mantle of the New York Yankees;
"The Mick," one of my boyhood idols.

GASPING FOR BREATH

At fourteen, like other kids my age, I drew inspiration for my actions and ambitions from the adult role models in my life. Most of these came from the world of sports. Endicott's two greatest names—E-J's George F. Johnson and IBM's Thomas J. Watson Sr.—were not only not high on my list of heroes, they weren't on the list at all, despite the pre-eminence they'd achieved in their respective fields of endeavor. Besides, both were deceased, and dead people didn't count for much.

Johnson had died in November of 1948, one month and two weeks after his ninety-first birthday. Watson, founder of IBM, had passed away in June of 1956 at the age of eighty-two, only about one month after turning the stewardship of his company, which he'd run for more than forty years, over to his son, Thomas J. Watson Jr.

George F. Johnson and the elder Watson had both figured prominently in Endicott's rapid ascendancy as an industrial juggernaut. In my mind, however, they were virtual non-entities. They didn't wear pinstripes, they didn't fight fires, they didn't kill "Japs" on the big screen at the Elvin Theater like Audie Murphy. Worst of all, they were dead.

Had I been better versed in their respective histories, I might have held the village's two most famous adopted sons in higher regard.

Johnson, I discovered later, was much like myself as a boy back in Milford, Massachusetts. A strapping, blue-eyed, red-haired kid, he was an above-average pitcher who didn't care much for studying. He didn't like attending Sunday School in the church in which his mother, a devout Methodist, worshipped, and he had difficulty suppressing the wanderlust he felt tickling the balls of his feet. He even toyed briefly with the idea of going to sea on a whaling vessel. Instead he took a job in a boot-making factory in nearby Ashland, Massachusetts.

I would have been impressed with the incident that, perhaps more than any other, prompted a young George F. Johnson, who already had a streak of fair play in him, to become a humanitarian and a philanthropist. Working one day at a bench in "Seaver's cellar," an Ashland, Massachusetts boot shop, where his duties consisted of chopping soles and heels from dirt-caked, discarded boots for three dollars a week, Johnson came across a two-dollar bill in the toe of one of the boots. "Look what I found!" he yelled to a co-worker. "Here—what's this?" the stern voice of the shop's boss called over Johnson's shoulder. "Boy, don't you know everything that comes in here belongs to *me?*"

This early introduction to the kind of corporate greed that would eventually become the modus operandi of many CEOs in America turned Johnson's stomach. He decided on the spot to seek a different job in the shop. He also vowed that if he was ever in a supervisory position, or fortunate enough to own a company, he would treat his workers better. Almost exactly fifty years later, three hundred miles to the west, on "George F. Day," with a mist hanging in the air in the aftermath of overnight rain, and with the E-J Workers Band performing Auld Lang Syne, the "E-J Workers Arch" was dedicated in George F. Johnson's honor. On that day—Labor Day, 1920—the notion of the village of Endicott,

New York as "the Home of the Square Deal" was cast in stone. Literally. With the christening of the E-J Workers Arch, residents and visitors alike were provided with a permanent reminder that, if you worked for E-J, you got a decent shake.

Thomas J. Watson Sr.'s story was different, but equally compelling. Unlike George F. Johnson, he was not particularly athletic. This fact was reinforced when Watson made his annual pilgrimage to the first tee at IBM Country Club to hit the golf season's ceremonial first ball. Attired in street clothes and regular shoes, he would knock a dribbler fifty yards down the fairway, smile self-effacingly at the audience watching him from a respectful distance and then turn and walk back into the clubhouse. His official duties as a harbinger of the arrival of spring had been discharged. Now he could retire to the cafeteria, possibly there, over coffee and pastry, to share with associates his next extraordinary vision for IBM. His firm was already a leading maker of business machines; soon, it would acquire similar prestige with computers.

Like E-J's George F. Johnson, IBM's Thomas J. Watson Sr.'s career as a pillar of the free-enterprise system got its start in Endicott. IBM began its operations in the village not long after E-J had set down roots. About two decades earlier—in 1899—Harlow Bundy had launched the Bundy Time Recorder Company on Water Street in Binghamton. Mergers led to the formation of the International Time Recording and Tabulating Co. International Time Recording followed E-J to the new village of Endicott in 1905. Shortly thereafter, under the leadership of Thomas J. Watson Sr., the firm changed its name to International Business Machines: IBM.

The similarities between George F. Johnson and Thomas J. Watson Sr. extended to their penchant for reducing their philosophic approaches to doing business to a catch phrase. The one most commonly associated with Johnson was "live and help live." Johnson believed that a company's success was built on the premise that management and workers were striving toward a common goal, and that they should be united in purpose. Sometimes he referred to this as "going down the road together." He was always "out front" in his industry in his attempts to keep his workers content; he was ever cognizant of the fact that a happy worker is a productive worker. When, in 1916, in a bold but risky move, E-J became the first major local employer to reduce the work day of its labor force from nine to eight and a half hours, an "employee parade" was held in celebration! Twenty years later Johnson was still preaching labor and management togetherness to his employees. "We are glad," he wrote to his employees in 1936, "to see the spirit of E-J" still alive and well by way of workers "trying to help one another."

His letter continued:

"I have always thought that the old 'hyme' that seemed to come down through the ages—'Live and Let Live'—was a funny thing. So we substituted 'live and help live,' and the workers have subscribed to it, as a better title, set to a better piece of music.

" 'Live and let live.' The natural question: who coined that brilliant phrase in human relations? It is a great concession, isn't it? After you have 'lived,' to permit somebody else to 'live.' One wonders, what in the name of common sense would you do? Assassinate the fellow who is trying to 'live?' So 'live and let live' does not sound good to me. It is not a very magnanimous expression. 'Live and help live' sounds better. This is the E-J idea."

At E-J, "live and help live" evolved as the term that best described George F. Johnson's theories on enlightened leadership; at IBM, a phrase coined by Thomas J. Watson Sr. similarly became his corporation's battle cry. Just as "live and help live" was intended to generate among E-J workers a sense of mutual cooperation at all levels of the organization, one word—"think"— emerged as the term that most succinctly summed up IBM's philosophy. Unlike "live and help live," Thomas J. Watson Sr.'s "think" was meant to foster within the ranks of IBM's workforce a commitment to formulating infallible methodology. It was also designed to suggest that the employee who uses his or her brain to its maximum potential is the one most likely to generate bold ideas that IBM could turn into brilliant new cutting-edge technology. Around the globe, whenever the name "IBM" surfaced, it was inextricably linked with the word "think."

Although fully aware that George F. Johnson and Thomas J. Watson Sr. were the two individuals most responsible for Endicott's emergence as the "Charles Atlas" of "the Valley of Opportunity," I would not have been able to pass a history quiz on either man in the summer of 1960.

The New York Yankees were another matter. I had already begun teaching myself how to be a switch-hitter, like "No. 7," Mickey Mantle. With a thirty three-ounce bat in my hands and looking in the full-length mirror mounted to my mom and dad's bedroom door at the end of the hallway, I tried to emulate the Yankee slugger's slightly crouched stance. I did this from the right side and from the left. Outside, I'd swish the bat forward in a slow and menacing way in the direction of an imaginary pitcher just the way I'd seen "The Mick" do it so many times. "My forearms are almost as big as his!" I'd say to myself, wishing it was true. I could picture the ball sailing beyond the short "porch" into the right-field seats at Yankee Stadium, or rising majestically against a powder-blue sky and falling into the upper deck as the voice of Mel Allen, "Red" Barber or Phil Rizzuto carried the triumphant news to listeners over the radio: "Gone!"

My knowledge of the Yankees was encyclopedic; I could without hesitation rattle off the batting averages of all of the top players: Bobby Richardson; Elston Howard; Bill "Moose" Skowron; Tony Kubek; Hector Lopez; Roger Maris; Yogi Berra; Clete Boyer; Dale Long. I knew Whitey Ford's won-lost record and earned run average (ERA). Statistics on the Yankees poured out of my mouth faster than jokes from Red Skelton's.

Sports greats were not any harder to find at the local level. Endicott always had its share of superb athletes, including basketball players like John Shawkey. Shawkey was the first U-E cager over whom I "flipped." A brilliant shotmaker, he was good for twenty-five points a game even when weakened by the flu. On those infrequent occasions when I couldn't be in attendance at a U-E basketball game, I would tear open the newspaper the next day to check John Shawkey's line in the box score. Shawkey, to me, was the definition of a roundballer: lithe; quick; agile. He was poetry in motion as he angled to his right or left and then pulled up quickly to hammer home a field goal.

As a teen-ager, I followed the exploits of Ron Menichetti, another basketball player, and Dave Sammon, the football team's quarterback, with a religious devotion. Both were unassuming but solid performers. There wasn't a bit of showboat in either of them.

I watched Menichetti from the balcony of U-E's infamous old gym, "The Pit," where his soft looping shots from deep in the corners of the court, below, would swish cleanly through the netting as if guided there by radar. As a student at U-E, I'd look for him in the hallways. I mimicked his mannerisms. I even took to slipping my tongue under my bottom lip as I'd seen him do. It was probably a nervous gesture on his part, but I saw it as a habit to be envied—and replicated. I figured if I copied enough of Menichetti's moves, some of his skill as a round-ball standout would rub off on me.

Sammon was not a big kid and he was a tad flat-footed, but I loved his cool aplomb as U-E's QB. He'd march the team down the field with short bullet passes over the center or to the flanks, and I'd cheer lustily from my seat in the rickety wooden bleachers on the far side of Ty Cobb Stadium (the concrete stands on the near side would later become the "home" side). Sammon was the first in a long line of outstanding quarterbacks to wear the Orange and Black with distinction under Angeline's tutelage. Their names still leap off the pages of yearbooks and from yellowed newspaper clippings: Mickey Murtha; Randy Zur; "Fast Eddie" Koban; Fred Zappia Jr.; Angeline's own son Chris Angeline; Bart Guccia; Chris Waters. Their arms powered vaunted U-E teams of the 60's, 70's, 80's and early 90's.

Coach Angeline, once he got the engine to a full head of steam, had other tools at his disposal too. One—"no-huddle," or "race-horse," football—would drive opponents (and game officials) crazy. By repeatedly charging to the line of scrimmage before the other team could get set, the Tigers changed the whole rhythm of the contest, acquiring confidence and momentum in direct proportion to their rivals' increasing sense of exasperation. U-E used the tactic with a cold-hearted disdain for the havoc it would wreak on the game's flow and pace (the "chain gang"—the crew responsible for moving the markers—despised it). I reveled in its brilliance, and swooned in pleasure as enemy defenders scrambled to match up correctly. The "no-huddle" offense was one of the most lethal weapons in U-E's arsenal; opponents who came unprepared to face it paid a heavy price.

Amid the plethora of superheroes that were either directly or peripherally a part of my life, George F. Johnson and Thomas J. Watson Sr. were nothing more than distant visages. The Yankees captured much of my attention. During the summer of 1960 the "Bronx Bombers"—powered by the smoldering bats of Mantle, Maris, Berra and Howard—had drawn a bead on another American League pennant. Meanwhile U-E football fortunes were about to take a turn for the better. With my own matriculation at U-E set to begin, I needed no explanation for why I felt so good.

None of these individuals—not even Mickey Mantle—quite measured up to Grampa Lee. My grandfather may have been a squirt at about five-foot-seven, but he was a giant in my eyes. Knowing what a perfectionist and taskmaster he was around the

house after he retired from E-J, I had an appreciation for the grit
he must have brought to his job in the tannery. "Too small to sling
heavy hides around," the experts had supposedly said. He had
proven them wrong. His house and yard were a continuing reflec-
tion of a strong sense of purpose. No one ever kept an E-J home
better. No tool was out of place; not so much as a speck of dirt was
allowed to fleck its way onto the welcome mat.

On Saturdays, as I swept out the basement or the garage for him,
painted the white picket fence that stood between his driveway
and Mrs. Hawthorne's side yard, washed and vacuumed his car or
spread sawdust on his rose bushes, I could feel his presence close
by, watching my every move. More than once, rubbing polish
onto the chrome fenders of his car, I heard the inevitable squirt of
tobacco juice streaming toward the ground, and the words: "You
missed a spot, right there."

My grandfather believed that sawdust—preferably the variety
that fell in snowflake-sized pieces to the floor in the shop of my
Uncle Bob's mill as the whirring saws churned—was the key to
growing gorgeous roses, and he laid it around the base of his
plants periodically throughout the spring, summer and fall. He
was the first person I knew to employ sawdust as mulch, and to
have the same kind of trust in its capacity to produce miracles as
Rev. John Green, of the nearby West Endicott Baptist Church,
had faith in Jesus' ability to deliver us from the clutches of Satan.
My grandfather used sawdust, in fact, in all his flower beds. The
results were nothing short of spectacular. Whenever my parents
visited my grandfather's house, their first order of business was to
take a turn with him around the yard so that he could show off his
roses and rhododendrons.

Puttering around the house, my grandfather was all business. At
night, in the living room, he was a different person: animated,
carefree and relaxed. Friday nights, when the Lee men gathered
around the television to watch the flying fists of Floyd Patterson,
"Sugar Ray" Robinson, Ezzard Charles or Archie Moore on the

black and white television, my grandfather would slip into the kitchen to whip up a batch of popcorn. Just as my Uncle Stew had his own coveted recipe for spiedie marinade, Grampa Lee's formula for popcorn was a highly personal and yet simple one. He dropped a slab of bacon grease into a pan on the stove, melted it, poured a thin layer of Jolly Time kernels into the pan, covered the whole thing and shook the pan vigorously over medium-high heat. He repeated this process several times, transferring the popcorn to a large bowl when it was ready. Then he saturated it with butter and salt. How we survived this cholesterol overload is a mystery still to be solved; yet, both of my grandparents lived to an old age, showing no ill effects from the indulgence, and no member of my family was worse for having consumed the snack on a regular basis, as far as I can tell.

My grandfather's favorite pastime when we were all together in the living room was to walk to the closet at the bottom of the stairs, grab one of his felt fedoras, place it an angle on his balding head and begin prancing about like Charlie Chaplin. Sometimes he unleashed this routine in civilian clothes; sometimes he was in his pajamas. To this act he would add jokes or comical faces as he shuffled from one person to the next, leaving me, as I got older and became more self-conscious, filled with a sense of dread as I awaited his arrival squarely in front of me.

How briefly, in the long sweep of time, the luxury of such an existence as the one I enjoyed as a youth endures! Eventually I would recognize that nothing lasts forever, that much is not as it seems, and that sunshine is invariably mixed with rain. That's life. These lessons would come in different ways. From my grandfather I learned diligence, patience and the value of humor and laughter. Other family members taught me other things. Stewart Lee taught me that few adults' love is mightier for a child than an uncle's for a nephew; he was encouraging and generous beyond measure. Unintentionally, he also taught me to resent the intrusion of the alcoholic person upon otherwise sober moments. By upsetting the equilibrium at home, at play and at work, he turned my affection for him to resentment.

At the ball game on Saturday, my uncle's good intentions had gone awry. Sunday afternoon brought a new "situation." After another night of drinking at the Sportsman's Inn and with his judgment knocked out of whack by the booze that coursed through his veins, my uncle chased Aunt Honey's car to the doorstep of our house, where the two of them arrived in a screeching cloud of dust and with the prospect of chaos charging the atmosphere. My aunt pulled up first. My uncle was right on her heels. My aunt darted across the front lawn. As my uncle gave chase, my mother slipped discreetly toward his vehicle, grabbed his keys and put them in the pocket of her apron, enabling my aunt to make an unimpeded escape. My father was assigned the unenviable job of calming my uncle down as my aunt drove off, shaken but uninjured. Their latest domestic spat was over.

Although the kickoff of the '60 season and "the Angeline years" at U-E lay just ahead, I was uneasy. Petty squabbling had already caused distress in my family. Uncle Ray, fed up with Uncle Bob's seeming lack of appreciation for his efforts on behalf of Lee Window, had broken away to form a new home-building firm. My dad would eventually do the same. Meanwhile, the time was drawing near for the wrecking ball to crash upon E-J's buildings on North Street. Soon, the symbols of Endicott's greatness would be reduced to ruins. Many of the glorious remnants of George F. Johnson's empire had already disappeared from the landscape or were about to slip into oblivion. The demise of Washington Avenue—the village's and the area's pre-eminent shopping district—would follow.

Endicott had been known far and wide as "the Valley of Opportunity" because of its shoemaking factories, IBM's facilities and the village's thriving downtown. Now E-J and Washington

Avenue were on the precipice of doom, even as fervor was build-ing in anticipation of a bright new chapter in the annals of "Tiger Town" football.

There was no way to freeze the village in time, or to save it from certain calamity.

A powerless teenager, I had to stand by and watch as Endicott disintegrated before my very eyes: brick by brick, building by building, place by place.

Shoe Town U.S.A. was dying.

The building that housed our hometown newspaper, the *Endicott Daily Bulletin*, which ceased publication in 1960.

"Cy," Courtship & Cider

My friend and self-appointed bodyguard Cyrill "Cy" LaBare from E. Wendell Street in West Endicott guided my safe passage through Jennie F. Snapp Junior High School, where I spent the seventh, eighth and ninth grade. A tall, muscular kid with a slightly pocked faced who had already begun to shave, Cy was often mistakenly thought to be at least twenty years old. Until then, I had never met anyone more physically intimidating than two toughs I'd grown up with in West Corners: Rick Biko and Larry Conklin.

Rick and Larry's reputations as brutish individuals who would not hesitate to break heads if they did not get their own way were deserved. They lived a few streets apart near the creek along Route 26 and were inseparable, like a pair of bookends. They called the shots in lower West Corners with a Godfather-like malevolence toward those they disliked, or who showed the slightest sign of insubordination or weakness. As a result, the rest of us stepped lightly when in their company, or bowed to their every demand. They were genuine street scrappers who could back up their threats with fists that dealt pulverizing punishment.

Next to Cy LaBare, however, they seemed like a couple of choir boys.

The asphalt playground along the solid-brick north side of the hulk-ing junior high school building on Loder Avenue in Union was Cy's private domain, and he savored his standing as lord of the manor. In the mornings before first bell and at lunch time, students would gath-er to throw a hard rubber ball high against the side of the building, then scramble for position in an attempt to catch the object as it smacked overhead and caromed back to them. This gathering includ-ed some of the most dexterous, quick-footed, strong and enterprising youth Union, West Corners and West Endicott could muster for such an activity. Regardless of how much pushing and shoving and elbow-ing took place, however, the ball always seemed to wind up in Cy's oversized mitts. Time after time this ritual repeated itself, usually with the same result. Cy controlled the action. Between the several inch-es he had on the rest of us and the knack he'd acquired for gauging exactly what speed and height were required for the ball to return to the same spot from which he'd launched it, it was as if he was playing a game of catch with himself. This didn't stop us from trying, in the vain hope that "one of these times," we'd get lucky.

Frequently, during gym-class softball games that took place in one corner or the other of the playground, Cy would lift a high fly ball toward the sky. Then he would stand at home plate for several sec-onds, like Barry Bonds of the San Francisco Giants does today, watching in satisfied self-absorption as the round white ball contin-ued its upward trajectory. He would smile from ear to ear as the ball finally landed with a thud on the roof of the school, a few hundred feet away. Recognizing the enormity of the accomplishment, the rest of us would shake off our shock just in time to raise a loud "yeah!" in collective praise as Cy loped around the bases. After Cy had lost sev-eral softballs in this fashion, three or four of his fellow students, accompanied by a gym teacher, would venture onto the roof through a hatch inside the school to retrieve the balls. This was one of the highlights of my years at Jennie F. Snapp. I viewed the sense of empowerment I felt as a "chaser" of Cy's tape-measure shots as the next best thing to having struck the blow myself.

By the time I'd reached the ninth grade at Jennie F. Snapp (the school was named after a revered long-time teacher and principal), my circle of friends had widened considerably. Besides the cronies who lived or hung out in West Corners that I'd counted as buddies for years (Chuck Mitchell, Bobby Muir, Tom Giordano, Tom Morris, Kevin Cahill, Joe Tingley and Joe's cousin Lee Vanderpool), my entourage came to include a number of new acquaintances. Many of these resulted from my tempestuous liaison with Laurene Perfetti.

Throughout junior high and high school I would encounter individuals whose appearances, idiosyncrasies or personalities distinguished them from the crowd. Tom "Dink" Demkovich was one of these. Dink, a short, slight kid with a full head of wavy hair, was like a character plucked from the set of "Grease." He was the ultimate schoolboy "punk." Dink compensated for his lack of size and stature by affecting an "I'm-with-it" attitude. In Dink's case, the ruse worked. He acquired friends as if picking cherries. He was fun to be around. Everyone loved him. Everyone except our teachers, that is. By always acting up in class, he made their life difficult. To his peers, however, Dink was a "dude." He was totally hip. He wore "white bucks!" No one dressed better. No one told jokes better. No one smoked better. No one undressed girls with his eyes better. Dink was a guy you had to know.

The 1959-1960 school year was a banner one for me. Every day after school Perfetti and I, accompanied by Pat Steenburg, Penny Chetko, Josie Shady and a few other friends, would walk with our arms draped around each other to her house on Wilma Street in West Endicott. The slow pace we set as we ambled west through downtown Union and past the tidy homes on Main Street afforded ample opportunities for kissing and necking. When I tried out and made the freshmen basketball team a couple of months into the school year, my status as a member of the "in" crowd was cemented. I was now officially a "jock," with all the advantages and benefits that title affords.

I can still feel the tingle that ran up and down my arms and spine when I trotted onto the court at Jennie F. Snapp Junior High with the rest of the frosh basketball team. We were the chosen few, the twelve of us who had been picked to wear the school's colors in action, and my chest burst with pride as, turning away after dropping a lay-up during pre-game warm-ups, I spotted Perfetti shouting encouragement to me from the sidelines. Students and teachers migrated in small groups down the hallway to the gym for those weekday-afternoon games. By the time the game tipped off, the far side of the court was packed with supporters. I hungered for the chance to show my stuff to an audience; the day I came off the bench to sink three field goals for six points was all the proof I needed that I was an emerging superstar. My heart was beating in rhythm to the clapping that rang in my ears.

The relationship between Perfetti and I was at a fever pitch and getting hotter by the minute. Afternoons alone in her living room and nights at house parties at friends' homes, our attraction to one another grew more passionate. One night, slow dancing with Perfetti in the corner of a dark room at Gretchen Boardman's house, I unbuttoned her blouse; at that moment, we were as close as we'd ever been to going all the way. Consumed by an intense want everywhere we went, we teetered on the edge of consummating the matter in one burst of abandon. Perhaps because something told us this would amount to social catastrophe, we stopped short. Meanwhile my mother, overcome with concern about where we were headed, had begun a campaign to dose the flames. "She's Catholic, we're not," she'd tell me. To this she added, as if by way of training additional ammunition on the target, "Italian girls always go fat when they get married." These admonitions falling like hammer blows did nothing to cool my jets for Perfetti. It wasn't until after arriving at U-E, where forces beyond our control exerted a new and powerful influence on each of us, that Perfetti and I finally called it quits.

— ❖ —

Looking back, "everything looked better in black and white" (as I heard a man say recently in describing the 50's and early 60's). Color television and other advances hadn't yet come along in full force, like waves cresting one after another, to alter our splendid routine. My own life was uncluttered and yet bountiful. The leisurely days I'd spent at West Endicott Park during the summer of 1960 had convinced me that the fun was just beginning. Riding the carousel with a Tootsie pop or Fireball in my mouth, spinning round and round in fantasyland as the band organ blared its pleasant tunes, hopping from one horse to another and dismounting before the ride had come to a stop (in defiance of the rules), I was sure the good times would continue to flow.

I was leaving Jennie F. Snapp Junior High School and downtown Union and would miss them. Bobby Muir and I had eaten many a lunch at Ken's, on Nanticoke Avenue. Perfetti and I and our friends had been regulars at both the Elvin and State theaters in Union for several years. The petting in which Perfetti and I engaged in theater seats that we'd purposely chosen because they were situated far from the main aisles and thus mostly out of range of the usher's flashlight was more torrid than anything depicted on the big screen. Most of the clothes I wore came from either the main floor or the basement of Vaughn's Men's Shop at the corner of Main and Nanticoke in Union, where my mother had a standing account. Streamers, horns and other gadgetry for my bike were purchased at Beaches Cycle Shop on the south side of Main Street in Union; Mr. Beach could often be found in the alleyway at the rear of the store, "wrenching" a bicycle back into working condition. On rare occasions I had been able to get a peek inside the Moose Club at the intersection of Loder Avenue and Main Street in Union, just east of the business center. All sorts of rumors swirled about what kind of goings-on took place there. The Moose Club featured massive white columns in front and a grand front porch. It had once been the home of Lawrence Mercereau, whose family was identified with many of the affairs of the town throughout the early years of its development. Built in 1830, the Mercereau home later succumbed to the wrecking ball, as did so many of Endicott's signature properties; it is now the site of a Pizza Hut restaurant, of all things.

As a boy I was quite taken by two buildings on North Street. North Street, formerly Railroad Street, ran generally parallel to Main Street a few blocks north of Main, and ended at Nanticoke Avenue. One of these buildings was the train depot for the New York and Erie Railroad. The other was the Union Forging Co. plant, just east of the depot. It was well known that Daniel Webster had come to town to help dedicate the train depot around 1849. Union Forging, meanwhile, had been in operation since about 1883. It had served the country nobly in a defense-contractor capacity during both world wars. The din created by the trains roaring past the depot and the racket that could be heard through the half-opened windows of the Union Forging Co. building were music to my ears.

As I left Jennie F. Snapp in the spring of 1960 and prepared for transfer to U-E High School, I looked forward with a renewed delight to a practice my friends and I had established. From West Corners, West Endicott and Union on Saturday mornings in the fall, we would converge on the Ciotoli family's Cider Mill on Nanticoke Avenue in Union and load up on cider and fresh doughnuts before beginning the trek to Ty Cobb Stadium, a couple of miles away, for Tigers' home games. Setting out from the Cider Mill had become a ritual. Just as the U-E players queued up in the clubhouse at Ty Cobb Stadium before home games, we considered it our sacred duty to meet first at the Cider Mill. It was our good-luck charm.

The Cider Mill's Tony Ciotoli Sr., who'd worked for Endicott-Johnson, ran several businesses out of the historic three-story red barn-like building near the intersection of Nanticoke Avenue and North Street: first coal, then cider and after that as a distribution site for home heating oil.

We were spoiled to the core at the ages of fourteen and fifteen. Like West Endicott Park, En-Joie Park and downtown Union with its two theaters and Washington Avenue with its plethora of places in which to shop and hang out, the Cider Mill provided ample evidence that the children of Endicott had all of the best stuff at our fingertips.

How long could such a splendid situation last?

That year (1960), the *Endicott Daily Bulletin*, an afternoon newspaper, ceased publication from its offices at the corner of Main Street and Lincoln Avenue in Endicott. A broadsheet, it was the first newspaper I'd read. I relied on the *Endicott Daily Bulletin* for my baseball box scores and the scoop on what was happening in Union and Endicott. Its disappearance (it was absorbed by the *Binghamton Sun*, a morning paper) was like a kick in the stomach. It was a landmark in town. Its one-story building with the words "ENDICOTT DAILY BULLETIN" inscribed in block letters on the front had provided a degree of comfort, just as the newspaper, in my hands, had. And now the Bulletin was gone. Other staple institutions were about to vanish as well; none would be any more sorely missed than our beloved hometown daily.

There was no time to dwell on the loss of the Bulletin, however, not with my high school days just ahead. The previous fall, the freshmen football team had gone undefeated. Some of the stars of that team (my classmates John Dellos, Bobby Atkinson, Ken Pacioni) would now carry the torch forward at U-E under Fran Angeline.

September was fast approaching. Cider, candied apples, doughnuts dipped in confectionary sugar and football were just around the corner. Endicott was collapsing under foot; as far as I was concerned, however, the village was like the Rock of Gibraltar: indestructible. The opening game, against Binghamton North, was only a few weeks away. Optimism was in the air.

Coach Francis J. "Fran" Angeline of Union-Endicott High School:
fiery; flamboyant; and fabulously successful.

A "Welcome"
from "Coach" Nick

U nion-Endicott High School was as big and labyrinthine a
place as I had imagined. The three-story brick building was
even larger than Jennie F. Snapp. Aside from E-J's and IBM's manufacturing facilities, it was the most imposing structure in all of
Endicott. It seemed to grow out of the ground like a mighty oak
tree. Suitably, it had a whole corner to itself where Washington
Avenue, at its southern terminus, met East Main Street. Opened
in the early 1900's and expanded in 1924 to accommodate a
mushrooming student population, it was now home to several
thousand pupils. It was the place where young people from every
sector of the community—the village center, the North Side,
Union, West Endicott, West Corners, Glendale—came together
in one spot, under one roof, for the first time.

Compounding the sheer immensity of the building, which featured entrances on the east and west wings and from the front,
was a room-numbering scheme that I figured had been contrived
to leave awe-struck sophomores like myself completely befuddled.
I stumbled from floor to floor, and door to door, trying, futilely, to
find Mr. (Charles) Turver's biology class, or Mr. (Vito) Popelka's
room in Guidance, shaking my head in disbelief as I pondered my

ineffectual wanderings. Classmates, many of whom I'd never laid eyes on before, were similarly confused. With the clang of the bell signaling that it was time to change classes came a stampede down the hallways and stairs; as if, by quickening our pace, we could make up for our lack of familiarity with our new home.

A few weeks into the fall semester, slipping into gym shorts and a U-E Athletic Department T-shirt for gym class, I met Mr. Nicosia, and the rude awakening to which I'd already been sub-jected took on new meaning. I was dallying and goofing around, with no particular interest in venturing outside for that morning's prescribed Phys. Ed. ("PE") activity. Mr. Nicosia pounced without warning. In an instant my back had been slammed against the lockers and he was shouting in my face. "You want 'fun and games,' mister, I'll give 'em to ya!" he bellowed. A furtive glance at the eyeballs popping out of his head and the veins protruding from his neck was all it took to assure me that in the face of such uncontrolled fury it was in my best interests to proceed without further delay to my assigned place. From that day on, whenever I spotted "Nicosia" in the building or on the grounds, I veered cau-tiously to my left or right, or simply turned my head, rather than risk the humiliation of another public flogging.

A short but compactly built man with curly, thinning hair, Russ Nicosia compensated for his lack of size with a Napoleonic flair for physicality. He feared no one. In gym class and as an assistant coach with the football team, he projected an authoritarian air that earned him the attention—if not the complete admiration—of equals and subordinates alike. I was certain, in observing his machinations and gestures, that he would not back away from a fight even if the odds against him were 100 to 1. He possessed the heart of a lion and the instinct of a cat that has used up eight of the lives it has been accorded and is running out of options and resources.

Years later, after I'd left my job working for Bob Klink in the pro shop at Binghamton Country Club to become a sportswriter for

Ed Plaisted at the old *Sun-Bulletin*, on Henry Street in downtown Binghamton, and then for John W. Fox at the *Press & Sun-Bulletin*, on the Vestal Parkway in Binghamton, I encountered a more mellow side of Coach Nicosia. His role as a motivator and an enforcer for Coach Angeline notwithstanding, Coach Nick would greet me with a broad smile and a handshake when I followed the players' clattering cleats into the U-E clubhouse to obtain quotes on the outcome of the game. Out of courtesy, or more likely because he'd simply forgotten, he never mentioned the manhandling he'd given me the year I staggered my way into tenth grade. I also avoided the issue, on the premise that it is best to let sleeping dogs lie!

Interacting with Coach Nick on a professional level, I came to appreciate his infectious warmth, his spontaneous bursts of laughter, his quirky sense of the absurd and even his role as a disciplinarian and a taskmaster. He was, I concluded, an integral and invaluable member of a close-knit fraternity of coaches, players, teachers and supporters who collectively lifted U-E football to unprecedented heights during the Angeline years. The names of these various contributors grew as the Tigers' credentials swelled with each passing year. Even a partial calling of the roll is enough to take the breath away:

Dick Hover...Joe Marzo...Dan "Cott" Consol...Hank Vetter...Dr. Ted Nowicki...members of the Angeline family...Bob "Wurt" Wurtenburg...Dr. John Hudock...Anne Bennett...John and Peggy Villanti...Margot Kendrick...Joe Pisani..."Bucky" Picciano...Bill Gargano Sr...Mike Wesko Sr...Fred Zappia Sr...Fran Crooks... "Shorty" Bowen...Bob Gallagher...Dave Decker..."Grandma" Grace Hanley...Bob "Ozzie" Osbourne...Bart "Goosh" Guccia...Tony Romeo...Frank "Sarge" Sorochinsky...Bob "Beef" Adams...Ed "Fols" Foli...Randy Zur...Mickey Murtha...John "The Plow" Blishak...Supt. Richard "Mac" McLean...Dave Chernega...Joe Lucia...Bobby Norris...Al Pedley...Kirk "Corky" Barton...Gary Iacovazzi...John Pinto...Joe Roberto...Jim Truillo...Tom Mason...Monte Cole...Jim Bennett...Jerry Hanley...Dom Pisani...Rod

Zur...Dennis Belardinelli...Curt Parvin...Tom Fiori...Bob Veruto...Tom Mills...Gary Crooks...Lee Spadine...Ron Rejda...Mike Fabrizio...Mike "Moose" Longo...Charlie and Louise Zur...Nino Samiani...Bill "Doctor Mind" Hughes...Tom Bennett...Terry, Dom, Dan and Rich Hogan (the "Hogan's Heroes" brothers)...Mario Ciotoli...Dave Wolf...Loftus Hanley..."Fast Eddie" Koban...Tim Marsh...Gary Beddoe...Armie George; Dick Testa...Ken Tatko...Steve Villanti...Paul Norris...Gerry Bravi...Tom Breese...Ed "Duke" Decker...Maurice "Hammy" Hamilton...Frank "The Duke" Hoyt...Frank "Huggie" Huggins...Mike Miller...Tom "Mully" Mullins...Tony Rose...Wayne "T" Tidick...Vince Paniccia...Dino Dutcher...Larry "Hondo" Hanafin...Jason Marshall...Al Pedley...Alex Rita...Joe Mott... "Tank" Anderson...Brian "Juice" Jester...Greg Prusia...Kurt Felton...Supt. Dr. Bill Zimmerman...Rick Hover...Mike Crounse...Paul Munley Jr....Tom Pasquale...Mike Guarnieri...Rob "Bubba" Cole...Tino Fiori...Chris Rando...Steve Hover...Chris "Muddy" Waters...Jarvis Shields...Chuck "Chuckie Cheese" Loudon...Kerry Pedley...Dave Machalek...Marty Bortnick...Vito Popelka...Mary L. Pitkin...Frederica "Fritz" Hollister... Dave Adamson...Ben Prusia...Todd "The Load" Kelley...Matt Beers...Billy Carlini...Tony Valachovic...Mom Lea..."the Tigers' Pride Marching Band"...the U-E cheerleaders..."Harky" Dove...Lou Morris...Markus Wilson...Jeff Pilarcek.

This brotherhood—school administrators, coaches, players, equipment men, trainers, statisticians, family members, Endicott business persons and of course diehard Tiger fans of all ages and backgrounds—coalesced with one objective in mind: to inject Union-Endicott High School football with all of the muscle necessary for success. They received their inspiration and to a great extent their marching orders from Fran Angeline.

The evolution of this new army of devotees had begun with the naming of Angeline as coach. The timing could not have been more fortuitous so far as I was concerned: Angeline's arrival as coach and my own arrival as a student coincided, albeit purely by accident—a certain indication that the next three years were going to be the most memorable I had known. The staff, faculty and student body were gripped in a frenzy of anticipation as the new school year began to unfold; none of which made my pathetic stabs at "learning" the building any easier, unfortunately.

One of the largest high schools in the Triple Cities and the Southern Tier, U-E tended to swallow up the uninitiated. As had been the case when I arrived at Jennie F. Snapp, I felt insecure and lost in its cavernous innards. I knew it would take time to get acclimated. While I groped to find my place, Coach Angeline settled in as if sliding into his favorite easy chair. He had left to play football for Hal Lahar at Colgate. Then he had latched onto the coaching assignment at JC. Now he was back where he belonged, ready to revive the U-E football program.

The first test for Angeline and the '60 Tigers was fast approaching: the Indians of Binghamton North. No one could have predicted, at the outset of the '60 campaign, that Angeline would remain in place as coach for more than three decades, that the "roar of the Tiger" would echo across the Southern Tier once again, or that, come Saturday night, if the Tigers were playing a home game, all eyes in Endicott would turn toward Ty Cobb Stadium as the Orange and Black stormed en masse onto the field. I would become used to the feel of goose bumps on my arms as this spectacle unfolded. I would become accustomed to the sight of "the Orange tornado" thundering down the field. I would become adept at shifting my gaze from the action on the gridiron to the sidelines, where Angeline presented a captivating show of his own. He was like a restive volcano ready to erupt.

Most of all, I would become accustomed to victory.

Nothing less than victory would do.

George F. Johnson watching a ball game at Johnson Field in Johnson City, home of the Binghamton Triplets. Among his numerous achievements, Johnson helped bring professional baseball to the Triple Cities, paving the way for the arrival of such future Yankees as crafty southpaw pitcher Whitey Ford, fleet-footed outfielder Joe Pepitone and catcher Thurman Munson.

A New Era Dawns

As U-E's season opener against Binghamton North, and the dawning of "the Angeline era," approached, my run-in with Coach Nick faded in significance. The confrontation between us had been unsettling, but the pressing business of adjusting to a new building, new teachers, new classes, a new routine and a new atmosphere took precedence. Coach Nick, for all his bestiality, would have to get in line behind other things that commanded my attention.

Perfetti was enough to take my mind off even an individual of Coach Nick's domineering, intimidating persuasion. Laurene Perfetti was everything a suddenly sexually-motivated fourteen-year-old could hope to find in a girlfriend. She was in my opinion the finest example of flowering womanhood the village of Endicott had to offer in 1960: dazzlingly gorgeous; teasingly flirtatious; self-assured; precocious; eager to push our liaisons as far as our flirtations—and familial restrictions—would allow. I savored the feeling of masculine desire she provoked in me.

Throughout the summer, Perfetti had jockeyed for position with baseball—my first love. In this regard, the odds were stacked against her. The New York Yankees were never far from my thoughts as they drove for another American League pennant. I followed the exploits of the Bronx Bombers with the same devotion that my dad followed the ups and downs of the big names in professional boxing's heavyweight division. My father soaked up news of Floyd Patterson, Sonny Liston and Ingemar Johannson as if he were a cat licking milk from a bowl; in a similar manner, I scrounged the floor for any crumb of information I could find about Mickey Mantle, Whitey Ford and Yogi Berra.

The Yankees' AA (Eastern League) farm team, the Binghamton Triplets, who played their home games at Johnson Field, in Johnson City, deepened my affection for the game. I watched closely as Joe Pepitone—"the next Joe DiMaggio"—came through on his way "up the ladder." Pepitone was a "can't-miss" prospect at the minor-league level. He was sure and swift afoot and possessed an arm that cut down opposing runners from centerfield like a farmer felling wheat with a scythe. Dark and handsome, he was a power hitter who could spray the ball to all fields with authority. Much of the fanfare Pepitone generated among the scribes and the fans went straight to his head, however. Betrayed by a conviction that his ticket was punched for superstardom, he never realized his full potential in the major leagues.

Johnson Field was another gift from George F. Johnson. Sitting in the bleachers along the third-base line with my grandfather, my dad and one or more of my uncles, I was too caught up in the action unfolding on and off the field to know or care that George F. Johnson had brought minor-league baseball to the Triple Cities and that he had built the ballpark. Later in life, I would not have been surprised to learn this. Johnson's love for the game ran deep; his son, George W., shared George F.'s passion for the national pastime and was, like his father, an accomplished player. George W. Johnson made a name for himself as a member of factory and tannery teams in the Endicott area in the early 1900's.

As a youth I enjoyed an enormous command of the sport's lingo and vital statistics. I could pull the batting averages of Willie Mays

("The 'Say Hey' Kid") of the San Francisco Giants, Ernie Banks ("Mr. Cub") of the Chicago Cubs and Stan "The Man" Musial of the St. Louis Cardinals out of the air like a magician yanking rabbits out of a hat. I was not nearly as knowledgeable when it came to George F. Johnson's own exertions on behalf of baseball. After shepherding construction of Johnson Field to completion, and in order to concentrate on the production of shoes, Johnson had sold the franchise and then leased the field to the new owners for one dollar a year. This was his usual procedure: create a playground or a park and then turn it back to the community for the continued enjoyment of all. He'd done this time after time. He did it when he donated the reflecting pool in Recreation Park in Binghamton to the city in the 1920's. He did it with Johnson Field too. As was so often the case, his generosity did not end with the bequeathing of the ballpark; he continued to bear the costs of maintenance and improvements of Johnson Field.

Although I was ignorant at the time of Johnson's role in the creation of Johnson Field, I knew every square inch of the property it occupied in Johnson City. I had viewed games as part of "the Knothole Gang" that hung around on No. Broad St., just beyond the left-field fence. We'd take turns peering through cracks or tiny openings in the fence as we waited for brawny right-handed sluggers to loft a home run over the wall. Over the years, I had watched the action from the roofed grandstand behind home plate and from the first and third-base bleachers. I had observed with envy residents of homes that sat just past the centerfield fence, watching free of charge from their back porches. I had slapped my knees in delight in the third-base stands as my grandfather carried on a running dialogue with the blacks from Susquehanna Street in Binghamton. He and they seemed to speak the same language. They got along famously. They were especially adept at baiting the third-base umpire or the opposing team's third baseman in an attempt to determine if these people had "rabbit ears." The merriment generated by my grandfather and his unnamed friends was as good as any produced by the baseball clown Max Patkin when he visited Johnson Field to ham it up along the baselines, by flame-throwing softball pitcher Eddie Feigner of "The King and his Court" when he struck out batters from second base or pitched blindfolded or by the tomfoolery I had heard on the radio or seen on television involving Jack Benny and his sidekick "Rochester," Dean Martin and Jerry Lewis, Bud Abbott and Lou Costello or Amos and Andy. The frivolity and commotion that took place in that open grandstand, close to the third-base line, was the perfect sideshow to the pitching of Alfonso Downing and the long-ball swatting of Ken "Hawk" Harrelson: future major leaguers on their way up to "the Big Show."

No one was happier than me on September 3rd, 1960, when Don Lock—"the Kansas Clouter"—slammed his thirty-fifth home run of the season for the Triplets, against Springfield. No one was more tickled than me when I landed my first job in journalism as a sportswriter at the old *Sun-Bulletin* in 1966. In that capacity, I covered the Triplets from the press box with the likes of scorekeeper Len Terenzi and radio broadcaster Pete Van Wieren. Van Wieren later became a "voice" of the Atlanta Braves. I was thrilled at the prospect of climbing the ladder from the main grandstand to the press box, my scorebook in hand. I was tickled to call Johnson Field one of my "beats."

Within a few years, Johnson Field would be leveled to make way for a new highway (Route 17), dooming the Triple Cities to a life without professional baseball for the first time in decades. The loss of Johnson Field was another chink in the armor, another sign that the E-J years were over and not coming back. Johnson Field wouldn't have been considered any great shake of a ballpark like the minor-league stadiums that dot the nation today. In fact, it was rather homely. But it was a place I couldn't get enough of, like the merry-go-round at West Endicott Park and the pool at En-Joie Park. I wept unabashedly when the news swept the area that Johnson Field's days were numbered.

— ❖ —

The first few weeks of September, 1960 were a blur of action. It was all coming together as I started my sophomore year at U-E and the Tigers worked out at a torrid pace in anticipation of Angeline's debut as coach. The buzz in the village was all football. A single question was on the lips of engineers in the labs at IBM, tanners at E-J, cops patrolling The Avenue: could Angeline turn things around?

No one knew then what the next thirty-two years of "Tiger ball" would bring. No one knew what the '60 season would bring! That would all be played out in Technicolor on the field at Ty Cobb Stadium and on gridirons far and wide, as U-E began the process of resurrecting the powerhouse squads the school had become renowned for during the early years of the regime of "Ty" Cobb— Angeline's former mentor. Ahead were many surprises: the trade-mark "hurry-up," or "no-huddle" offense, which left so many of U-E's opponents dazed and confused; the introduction of the triple-option Wishbone attack, built around southpaw QB Tom Fiori, in 1974; the arrival of a string of sensational quarterbacks (Randy Zur, "Fast Eddie" Koban, Chris Waters); the emergence of a plethora of "tiny Tigers" who, year after year, would play over their heads in defiance of their physical limitations (six-foot, 185-pound defensive tackle Dave Machalek was a typical example); the speed game that prompted some to change the team's nick-name from Tigers to "Cheetahs;" the "Top Gun" offense; and so on.

Sitting in the concrete stands overlooking the green and noise-less field, waiting for the thunder to erupt a few days hence, my friends and I fretted about what the shoulder injury Bob Wheeler had suffered on the eve of the season would mean, and whether star senior end John Martgetanski would be at 100% coming off a chest injury. And those were not the least of our worries. U-E hadn't beaten Binghamton North since 1954 and Coach Gordie O'Reilly's Indians were riding an eight-game unbeaten streak.

Still hope flourished.

By the time he finished coaching in 1992, Angeline would amass 216 victories.

Would the first one come versus North High?

We couldn't wait to find out.

TOGETHER ON "THE AVENUE"

The people who shared The Avenue in Endicott at lunchtime in 1960 included blue and white-collared E-J and IBM workers, high school students from U-E and nearby Seton Catholic, village employees, and countless others. There was also a vagabond-like middle-aged man named "Windy" Gilroy. Even amid such an assortment, Windy stood out like a sore thumb. The mere shadow of his figure on the sidewalk in front of any of our hangouts was enough to cause a stir. Someone would either detain Windy long enough to get him started on one of his outlandish, rambling stories about worlds he had conquered—which invariably prompted a chorus of disbelief—or scream, "scat, your vermin, before we beat you to a pulp," in which case he'd scurry off in his customary stoop-shouldered shuffle, turning his head to shout epithets at his tormentors as he faded into the crowd clogging The Avenue.

Windy's haplessness, and the fact that he was outnumbered, made him an inviting prey for those who enjoyed heaping abuse on the defenseless. A mysterious, tiny man with a nervous tick who wore what appeared to be hand-me-down clothes, which drooped from his body, Windy was one of Endicott's and The

Avenue's legitimate oddballs. He was our chosen whipping boy. We had a love-hate relationship with him. Some days we'd gather round over cherry Cokes and slices of pizza, listen as Windy described what a hellcat he was in his youth and merely laugh in response; other days, in no mood for his tall tales, we'd run him out of the place before he'd gotten started. Regardless, he always came back, a glutton for punishment.

Only one other person I knew received anywhere near as constant a barrage of disdain as Windy Gilroy and that was Miss (Adona) Sick, the high school librarian. A spinsterish and unattractive woman with an authoritarian and generally disagreeable nature—and a decided lack of tolerance for the flightiness of youth—she was held in mutual contempt by most of the student body. When it came to punishing Miss Sick for her "crimes and misdemeanors" against young people, the boys were particularly unmerciful. Their favored form of retribution was to rain pennies at her from every direction. The pennies would land at her feet with a soft pitter-patter sound, like hailstones hitting the ground. Poor Miss Sick would turn her head sharply and with a piercing look scan the faces of the boys at the tables around the room in a determined attempt to identify the perpetrators: too late; all would by then be buried in their books—looking every bit as innocent as Rhodes scholars.

For those living and working in Endicott in the fall of 1960, Washington Avenue was the common denominator. George F. Johnson, Henry B. Endicott and most of the other founders of the village were no longer around to assess the merits of the street they had laid out more than half a century before, but it was fulfilling its early promise and then some. It had been a magnet for business people from the outset. In 1960 this was truer than ever. Along the stretch of pavement between Union-Endicott High

School and the E-J factories at the other end resided more businesses than you could shake a stick at. These businesses offered every product or service imaginable. It was as if George F. Johnson himself had sprinkled angel dust on a barren roadway back in the early 1900's and, puff, from the earth had sprouted a Monopoly board. It was a feast and everyone was invited to the table.

The growth of E-J and IBM fed the development of The Avenue. In the beginning, after workmen in wide-brimmed hats had graded it mostly by hand, The Avenue boasted trees on both sides of the street (these were eventually cut down, the first sign that The Avenue itself would ultimately shrivel and die). Initially there was only a sprinkling of buildings: the Endicott Market, operated by Anthony Dobrovolsky, which was one of the first businesses to open; the Hotel Frederick, which was erected in 1906 (the same year the village was incorporated); the Broad Street School, on Broad Street (which intersected The Avenue); and, between the Hotel Frederick and the Broad Street School the home of Capt. Francis A. Johnson (father of George F. Johnson). Soon to follow was the three-story Hotel Mix, on the eastern side of The Avenue at the corner of Monroe Street. The ground floor of the Hotel Mix would later become The Avenue Confectionary, arguably the most famous storefront on the street: a noontime eating place for Washington Avenue business people and a gathering spot for high school students come 3:30 in the afternoon. The Avenue Confectionary was owned by James Zades until his death, then Arthur Corino, then Frank and Helen Ferris who kept it going until it closed.

With the addition of trolley cars and then the paving of The Avenue in 1915 came an explosion of new businesses: the Cawley Novelty Shop; LaValle & Newing (a garage that also sold parts and accessories); bakeries run by William Duster and Fred Gallaway; four barber shops; three billiard parlors; two blacksmith shops; a stationery store owned by Louis Bacon; Shapiro's (one of an eventual total of seven clothing stores); four confectioners;

three drug stores; five dry-goods stores; a florist; two furniture stores; five groceries; three hardware stores; two jewelers; the U.S. Post Office; three banks; Cardilione and Iannone's fruit and produce store; three plumbing shops; three tailors; one undertaker; restaurants and saloons. Then Earl E. Padbury's taxicab office. Then the Ideal Theater and the Lyric Theater. Lawyers, doctors and dentists opened offices on The Avenue too.

Every time a business was lost, another stood poised to replace it. With the shuttering of the Lyric Theater came the arrival of the Strand, for instance.

By the early 1930's there were seven attorneys doing business on the street.

In its heyday, Washington Avenue boasted not one but three five-and-dimes: Neisner Bros., at 18-20 Washington Ave.; J.C. Newberry Company, at 32-36; and F.W. Woolworth Company, at 28-30. Two of these five-and-dimes had lunch counters. Two department stores (Burt's and McLean's) sold top-quality merchandise.

In the early 1960's, The Avenue personified a "Main Street" that America knew well. Few suspected then that mercantile meccas like Washington Avenue would ultimately disappear. From the time I first started trolling The Avenue as a young boy until I went away to college, I basked in its luxuriousness. Not once did I imagine that the places I frequented almost by habit on The Avenue would topple, one by one, like dominoes. And yet they did. By the 1970's and 1980's many of The Avenue's anchor businesses had closed their doors or relocated. Whenever I returned home for visits in the 1990's, I avoided the temptation to drive The Avenue from one end to the other on the simple premise that this trip down memory lane would leave me feeling despondent. Burt's and McLean's, gone. Woody's, gone. Zappia's, gone. The theaters, gone. The Avenue Confectionary, gone. Woolworth's, gone.

I experienced The Avenue not only as a pedestrian and a shopper but also as a busboy at the Hotel Frederick, where I cleared tables in the luxurious dining room at which U-E teachers and others liked to eat. When the Frederick was demolished, its owners had every intention of constructing a grand new hotel to replace it. Because of high building costs, that never happened, and the Frederick was lost for good.

So too, eventually, was the Main Street Grill, at the corner of Washington Avenue and Main Street.

E-J would leave, the historic buildings and beautiful En-Joie Park would be removed from the scene, IBM would later slip into a tailspin and lose thousands of jobs. The Avenue would hit the skids.

So much for my assumptions that Endicott, and Washington Avenue, would, like the willow tree in the side yard of our home on Hazel Avenue in West Corners, stand, undiminished, forever.

Rocker Fats Domino; "The Fat Man."

ROCKIN' & ROLLIN'

My favorite place on The Avenue was Woody's, a record store. Rock 'n' Roll's "Golden Decade" (1954-1963) was in full swing and had snagged the attention of the nation's teens. On the nightstand next to my bed, alongside the stack of baseball cards I had amassed, sat a small case for 45 RPM singles, and my turntable. I had purchased all of these records at Woody's. Day and night I would drop the disks onto the record player and listen, fixated, as the voices of Rock 'n' Roll's early greats filled the room.

I had been hooked on Rock 'n' Roll since watching Jerry Lee Lewis (a.k.a. "The Killer") tear into a rendition of "Whole Lot of Shakin" on Steve Allen's television show in July of 1957. The song had rocketed to No. 1 on the charts, and was followed by another big hit: "Great Balls of Fire."

I had never seen anyone like Jerry Lee Lewis. He brought the fury of a hurricane to the stage. The spectacle of Jerry Lee pounding the keys of the piano with his long fingers—with his knees and feet even—kindled in my bosom the first sparks of rebellion. Not long afterwards, convinced that the accordion, upon which I'd become proficient under the tutelage of Alex Apolovich, of Endwell, didn't cut it as a means of bold self-expression, I

111

informed my mother that I was abandoning the instrument. With that pronouncement came the end of my turns playing "The Beer Barrel Polka" and "Autumn Leaves" for small gatherings of acquaintances and relatives. My decision also dashed with a crushing finality my mother's hopes that I would emerge as an accordionist of stature in the mold of Myron Floren—from "The Lawrence Welk Show" on TV. The question of whether I would ever develop the silky-smooth technique Myron Floren exhibited every week would have to go unanswered.

With the release in 1960 of "Only the Lonely," by Roy Orbison, "Cathy's Clown," by the Everly Brothers, and "The Twist," by Chubby Checker, Rock 'n' Roll solidified its presence as a revolutionary force in America—and in the Lee household. By then I had accrued a set of singles that was the equal of any around (possessing, and playing them, was another way to lord my superiority as the older brother over my siblings).

Many of these 45's symbolized Rock's early youthful and innocent exuberance: "Blue Suede Shoes," by Elvis Presley; "Rock Around the Clock," by Bill Haley and His Comets; "Johnny B. Goode," by Chuck Berry; "Yakety Yak," by The Coasters; "Good Golly, Miss Molly," by Little Richard; "Ain't That A Shame" and "Blueberry Hill," by Fats Domino; "Calendar Girl" and "Happy Birthday Sweet Sixteen," by Neil Sedaka. Other artists' lyrics seemed to capture the heartbreak and mystery and restlessness that accompany adolescence.

U-E kids were able to tap several sources for the artists and records that spoke to the emotions we were feeling during our high school years: Dick Clark's "American Bandstand" TV show; the radio; and occasional live appearances by the musicians themselves—like Dion and The Belmonts, who I saw perform "The Wanderer," "Runaround Sue" and other songs at the old JC Rec in Johnson City.

To acquire actual vinyl copies of the records we wanted to hear, however, we turned to Woody's.

Like the Elk's Bake Shop, the Lyric (a theater), Zappia's (a sporting-goods store), United Men's and Boy's Wear (a clothing store),

Woolworth's (a five and dime store with a long, marble-topped lunch counter) and The Avenue Confectionary (an ice cream and soda shop), Woody's was a smash hit with the younger folks. A mere hole-in-the-wall of a storefront on the eastern side of The Avenue (next to Maddy's Music Centre), Woody's was always crammed with U-E High School and Seton Catholic High School students. Elbow to elbow, we'd finger through the sheathed LPs arranged in bins and the 45's that hung in paper sleeves on the wall. "Top 10" 45's were in constant demand. I emptied my pockets of one dollar after another to purchase the latest release from Del Shannon, Sam Cooke, Pat Boone or Ricky Nelson and to build my collection. I ran to Woody's in April of 1961 to buy Ricky Nelson's new single "Travelin' Man." The B side featured an equally compelling track: "Hello Mary Lou."

The days of cassette tapes and compact discs (CD's) hadn't yet come along. My friends and I kept pace with the swift-moving, brash new medium known as "Rock" by buying 33 RPM's—and especially 45's—as fast as the tracks were released by the record companies. We took them home. We carted them to house parties. We danced to them. We memorized the lyrics. Our "life of privilege" as residents of Endicott—where creampuffs, movies, cheeseburgers, pizza, blue jeans, sneakers, flannel shirts, yoyos and bargain-price necklaces and ID bracelets were always just a storefront away, on The Avenue—put us at a distinct advantage over kids in nearby towns who didn't have the same ready access to a shopping district that boasted a treasure chest of products and services. We took full advantage of our special circumstances by spending every spare minute we could on Washington Avenue, soaking up all that it had to offer.

Our exposure to the early "gods of Rock" spawned in my friends and me an appreciation for the music—and its messengers—that carried us through the decades that followed. We would graduate and drift off to different cities and towns. We would build lives that no longer touched one another. Rock 'n' Roll—and our memories of our years walking the halls of U-E, cheering for the Tigers and cruising The Avenue (on foot or at the wheel of a Mustang, Corvette,

Camaro or GTO)—were the thread that held us together: if only in a figurative sense. In short order Father Time would move in to claim his pound of flesh. All too soon our music would be pushed aside by the upstart sounds of Disco, Heavy Metal, Reggae and Rap. All too soon the voices of "My Generation"—Buddy Holly, Fabian, Johnny Rivers, Brenda Lee—would be able to be found only on the few stations on the radio dial gutsy (or foolhardy) enough to play "Oldies." And then these voices would almost completely fade from sight—a mere dot in the rear-view mirror.

In September of 1960, as the clock ticked toward U-E's opener against Binghamton North, schoolwork was the last thing on my mind; everyone else's, too, it seemed. The buildup to Fran Angeline's debut as U-E football coach had been intense; speculation about the Tigers' chances of victory surged through the village. At a pep rally in the auditorium of the high school a few days before the big game, Angeline—young, tanned from a summer spent in the sun, buoyant and oozing confidence and conviction—worked the student body into a state of near-delirium.

We were not to be disappointed. On Saturday, September 24th, 1960, U-E beat North for the first time since 1954, 13 to 6. In doing so, the Tigers also snapped the Indians' eight-game unbeaten streak. It was an auspicious start for Angeline, who prowled the sidelines, clipboard in hand, like an unleashed Tiger. In the stands, we couldn't relax until deep into the fourth quarter. U-E had taken a 7-6 lead in the second quarter when George Wallace, on his second crack at the North defensive line, scored on a one-yard plunge and Ed Ciotoli kicked the extra point.

I was convinced that a classmate of mine, John Dellos, a quiet kid who'd quarterbacked the freshmen squad to an undefeated season in '59, was U-E's QB of the future. It was the current QB, however, who rose to the occasion against North. Dave Sammon, always cool and collected, led the Tigers on a 51-yard march late in the game and crossed the goal line himself from the one-yard line to complete the scoring. Still U-E fans could not relax. Not until Carl Harder intercepted a pass thrown by the North quarterback, Ray Stanton, at the U-E 15, nullifying the Indians' last-gasp threat, did we sense that victory was in hand. After Harder's heroics came even more theatrics that left us squealing in appreciation: Dick Pugh, who together with fellow lettermen like George Wallace and Dick Vivona had been tabbed as one of the keys to a successful '60 season, broke a 69-yard run around right end.

Bedlam erupted on the U-E sidelines. Win No. 1 of the Angeline era was in the books. Soon enough, victory after victory would follow. It would quickly become apparent to residents of Endicott that if anyone was destined to spend a near-lifetime in the game of football, it was Fran Angeline. Determined and hard working, he had cracked the U-E starting lineup as a sixteen-year-old; that same season, he was also named a Southern Tier Conference (STC) All-Star at end. He had gone on become a captain of the football squad at Colgate University, in Hamilton, New York. He had remained at Colgate as an assistant coach while earning his Master's degree. He had returned to the Triple Cities to become a head coach—at the age of twenty-two—at Johnson City High School. Then came the call from his high school alma mater—U-E—and the return to Tiger Town: the start of a football odyssey that would rival any the area had seen.

Next up for the Tigers as September of 1960 drew to a close was Johnson City: the very school Angeline had left earlier in the year in order to come back to U-E. Again the challenge seemed immense: U-E hadn't beaten the Wildcats since '53. And there was the disaster of the previous year's collision to consider, when the 'Cats, powered by the play of Bill Baker, Tony Fusco and Gerry Kocak, had run up a 27-0 lead on the Tigers en route to a lopsided win.

This time, things would be different.

I was certain of that.

Grandma and Grampa Blossom (James F. "Jim" and Blanche Blossom).

Uncle George and Aunt Peg (George and Margaret Hallberg).

THE PIG STAND—
AND A LOSS

Major decisions involving family matters were usually made around the dining-room table at our home on Hazel Avenue in West Corners. Occasionally the setting for such judgments shifted to my grandparent Lees' house in West Endicott or to my grandparent Blossoms' house in Apalachin ("over the river and through the trees"). My Grandma Blossom—Blanche Blossom—liked bringing God's Word, as interpreted by the Rev. John Green of the West Endicott Baptist Church, whose teachings she considered to be unassailable, into any discussion upon which momentous consequences rested. Whether the issue was dancing (taboo), drinking, smoking, cursing, going to the movies, pre-marital sex or working on the Sabbath (all also forbidden), the guidance provided by the Bible, the Baptist faith and Rev. Green was law.

I resented having to traipse to Birdsall Street in West Endicott for Wednesday-night prayer meeting in addition to Sunday school and Sunday-morning worship. Sometimes we went back to church for Sunday-night worship too! It was almost worth it, however, to hear Grandma Blossom's voice raised to the rooftops as she sang "The Old Rugged Cross" or "How Great Thou Art." My grandmother loved "that old-time religion." She quoted passages from

The Good Book to deal with any ailment or circumstance, said grace over meals and played hymns on the piano. In her younger days she implored the Lord to protect her when picking strawberries on rattlesnake-infested hillsides in Pennsylvania.

"I never worried," she told me in relating descriptions of such outings—and a possible encounter with a venomous bite. "God was with me."

Grandma could laugh like there was no tomorrow. In that regard, she offered a welcome contrast to my stern grandfather, Jim Blossom, who my brothers and I seemed to irk no matter how hard we tried to behave—and to stay out from underfoot.

Because we spent many Friday or Saturday nights pulled up in front of Grover's Pig Stand, just over the Endicott line in Endwell, a lot of family matters were also aired and brought to a resolution there. The Pig Stand had a dining room but most customers, taking advantage of carhop service, ate outside—at the curb. I looked forward to forays to the Pig Stand for two reasons: the food, which always measured up; and the female carhops. The girls brought the trays to the driver's-side window of my dad's Desoto. They were slightly older than me, and deliciously appealing in their short skirts.

I knew without being told that the Pig Stand was one of the Endicott area's prime addresses. It seemed as if we had so many: most if not all attributable to George F. Johnson's influence. The church I attended was one of them. In 1927, Johnson had donated land at the corner of Birdsall Street and Mills Avenue in West Endicott so that a new home for the church—originally named the Tabernacle Baptist Church of West Endicott—could be built. He also contributed lumber and other materials. The old wooden house of worship in which a small congregation had met was razed. A new edifice went up. By the time I took my appointed place in a pew between my parents and grandparents near the front of the sanctuary for the first time in the late 1940's, the church's name had changed twice: it became United Tabernacle Baptist Church of West Endicott upon merging with Emmanuel Baptist. In October of 1948 it became West Endicott Baptist Church. Without Johnson's generosity this sequence of events might never have occurred. If not for that initial boost from Johnson, West Endicott Baptist probably would not have jelled as an institution like it did. Beginning in the early 1950's and continuing through the late 1980's, the unpretentious box-like structure underwent a series of upgrades. Sunday-school rooms were added. An auditorium and a gymnasium were built. Then the auditorium was remodeled.

George F. Johnson's goodness notwithstanding, West Endicott Baptist Church was not a place I liked to frequent. Exercising my rights of deception at the ages of eight and nine, I would, upon being dropped off for Sunday school by an adult, walk toward the outside steps leading to the basement classroom—and then, as my "chauffeur" pulled away, sneak off with a couple of cohorts. We would dart toward the nearby candy store and loiter there, sucking down licorice and watermelon candy, until just before eleven o'clock. Then we'd suddenly materialize again, discreetly working our way into the crowd of older folks gathered in the vestibule of the church. At that moment, we would try to look innocent even though we were as guilty as sin.

West Endicott Baptist Church was low on my list when it came to haunts. As a destination, it could not hold a candle to the En-Joie pool, West Endicott Park, the Endicott Boy's Club or The Avenue. I needed interesting, not boring. Throughout my boyhood, I had pestered workers breaking up big blocks of ice in front of Magic City Ice Co. for chips to pop into my mouth on hot summer afternoons. I had scoured the slopes of Round Top for secret caves of the sort F.W. Dixon had described in the Hardy Boys books; I had searched for Indian arrowheads there too. I had rummaged the banks of the Susquehanna River and the Nanticoke Creek for frogs and minnows and snakes. I had devoured every sports book I could put my hands on at the George F. Johnson Memorial Library. I had consumed large quantities of cider and doughnuts from the Cider Mill. I had dreamed of being a detective or a bon vivant or a cowboy while watching Cary Grant, Rock Hudson and John Wayne at the Elvin Theater. I had licked many an ice-cream cone into submission while sitting on the concrete wall bordering the cemetery just a few steps away from Pat Mitchell's. I had studied the movements of the great local baseball and softball players from the bleachers at the Page Avenue Field. I had looked on—maintaining a safe distance—as Sam Bevilacqua and Frank Ambrose operated the sharp, high-speed saws in the shop at my uncle's mill.

The largely laborer populace of Endicott at that time did not need fancy restaurants when it came to eating out on Friday or Saturday night. A family of five could obtain good grub at Grover's, in Endwell—or Fusco's, in West Endicott—for about twenty dollars.

The Pig Stand was not in Endicott, but Endicott claimed it as its own. My family's order after we'd pulled into the parking lot seldom varied: five pork-barbecue sandwiches; three root beers; a couple of cardboard containers of fries and two cups of coffee. Maybe it was the food, but everything seemed to smooth out when we got to Grover's. All of the week's tension disappeared. Sitting in the car, waiting for our tray to be brought out, we occupied ourselves with small talk about family, school and work. The minutes passed. By the time our meal arrived, we were relaxed—and hungry.

Once in a while, Grover's was summoned into service as a destination at which big breaking news was delivered. This was the case one afternoon in the spring of 1964 when my father piled my brothers and me into the car. "Let's go to the Pig Stand," he said. En route, he told us that my mother was expecting a fourth child. My mom was thirty-nine years old. I was a year out of high school. Randall Howard "Randy" Lee arrived that October.

Grover's boasted a diverse menu, but pork-barbecue sandwiches were its forte. I can still taste them. They were simple fare compared to the elaborately concocted fast-food sandwiches of today-

and yet in a league of their own. They consisted of pork sliced razor thin and piled high on a steamed bun. The meat was topped with a special sweet relish sauce. For years after Grover's shut down, whenever I spotted a BBQ beef or pork sandwich on another restaurant's menu, even restaurants far removed from Endicott, I would order one—hopeful that I had rediscovered long-lost treasure. I am still looking.

At Grover's that last Friday night in September of 1960, my father listened with his customary patience to my continuous barking from the back seat of the family car about the Tigers' prospects against Johnson City the next afternoon. He was well aware of the unusual drama involved; our new coach, Fran Angeline, would be butting heads for the first time with the man who replaced him on the sidelines at JC: Henry "Hank" Diller.

We were coming off the triumph over Binghamton North, the details of which were still fresh in my mind. I was convinced that a second straight win was imminent, and that fellow members of my sophomore class would play an increasingly pivotal role in the Tigers' fortunes as the season progressed.

Several of the "Italian Stallion" athletes new on the scene were going to emerge as standouts, I told my father. One of these was Ken Pacioni. I had already become friends with Pacioni in the hallways at U-E. Most of the students had, in fact. He was the kind of guy you couldn't help but like: warm and engaging. His accommodating demeanor masked a meaner streak, though. What Pacioni lacked in size—he weighed just one hundred eighty pounds—was offset by an expression that turned foreboding when he lined up at tackle. There, he'd already established himself as a presence. Over the next three years at U-E, Pacioni would endear himself to the most nondescript, low-ranking members of the student body: he was that easy-going and chummy a guy. He would also prove to be a formidable performer in the trenches on the football field. Ken Pacioni—No. 61—was one to watch, I told my father. His talents as a blocker and tackler, his love for the game and his ferociousness when the whistle blew would imbue the Tigers with a new sense of purpose. I was sure of this. Angeline apparently thought so too. He had already identified Pacioni to the media as one of several newcomers from the standout '59 frosh squad capable of earning a starting slot on the varsity team.

In talking up players like Ken Pacioni, Joe Conrad, Mike Nalavenko, Bobby Atkinson, Dick Streno, Vic Battaglini, Jerry Niles, Ted Liburdi, Joe Nejeschleba and John Dellos to my father, I was reinforcing a hunch my dad and the rest of Endicott already had that U-E football teams, under Angeline, would rebound from years of mediocrity and reclaim the school's rightful place as kingpin of the gridiron in the Triple Cities and the Southern Tier.

The turnaround wouldn't come quite so soon, as it turned out. JC, like North, presented a formidable challenge for the Tigers. The sportswriters were quick to observe that JC hadn't lost to U-E since 1953. Furthermore, the mainstays of the Angeline-coached JC team that had manhandled U-E the year before were back for another year: Bill Baker, Tony Fusco and Gerry Kocak.

Finally, it was Game Day.

That U-E "came to hit," as John W. Fox put it in his story in the *Binghamton Press* on Sunday, did not take much of an edge off the bitterness the U-E student body was feeling in the aftermath of the 15 to 6 loss the Tigers suffered the previous afternoon. We had piled into buses for the short ride up the George F. Highway to Johnson Field (where, like the Triplets' baseball team, JC played its home games), confident that win No. 2 of the young season was just a few hours away. We had pigged out on cider and doughnuts and then waved Orange and Black pompoms out the windows of the buses as we rolled through downtown Johnson City and turned left to cross the viaduct that took us down to Johnson Field. We sang fight songs. We were giving Johnson City a good dose of Tiger spirit.

Great victories and remarkable seasons lay ahead for Angeline and the Tigers: successive lopsided wins in '64, for instance, over Elmira Southside (34-0), North (49-0), Binghamton Central (55-0) and Ithaca (33-7). There would be the clamor that arose in '79 when the Tigers demolished one opponent after another inside and outside of the conference: Buffalo's Sweet Home, 47-0; Norwich, 34-0; Central, 78-0; North, 63-14; Susan B. Wagner High of Staten Island, 34-6; JC, 55-6; Maine-Endwell, 51-0; Ithaca, 35-0 and finally Vestal, 16-0. That year—1979—the Tigers set individual and team records right and left, and were ranked No. 1 in the state of New York by the New York State Sportswriters Association (NYSSA).

There would follow a 21-15 win over Rome Free Academy in 1980 in a battle of state-ranked teams; a 24-6 victory over Binghamton in 1986 to snap the Patriots' 21-game win streak; a 9-0 season in '89, including a 21-19 win over Corning East in the Section 4 Bowl 1 game at Cornell University's Schoellkopf Field that featured long TD runs by Markus Wilson (61 yards), Jarvis Shields (77 yards) and Paul Norris (28 yards).

The JC game of 1960 would not be one of these.

Among the things to brag about that afternoon was a breakthrough performance by an until-then little-used 164-pound senior: Bobby Colburn. A former defensive end, Colburn, who was slender, shifty and resilient, rushed ten times for forty-five yards. U-E fans erupted when Colburn broke a punt or kickoff return.

Still the Tigers lost.

"Not to worry," I told Bobby Muir as we re-boarded the buses for the somber return ride home to Endicott. "We'll destroy Ithaca."

Actually, I wasn't so sure.

Laurene Perfetti; the first love of a romantic teenager's life.

AGONY AND ECSTACY

September gave way to October. Warm summer nights yielded, begrudgingly, to fall's encroaching chill: apropos, perhaps, of the cooling of passions between Laurene Perfetti and me. We had been going steady since seventh grade. We had been a couple throughout our junior high school years. Our friends, cognizant of our intense feelings for one another, would have sworn that our clasp could never be broken. At Jennie F. Snapp Junior High School, the student body assumed—appropriately enough, given the circumstances—that the blond, lightly skinned basketball player from West Corners and the darkly complexioned social butterfly from West Endicott would remain boyfriend and girlfriend forever, no matter what. Like Frankie Avalon and Annette Funicello from Walt Disney's "The Mickey Mouse Club:" a match so perfect that nothing could come between us. Not even high school and its attendant pressures.

It ended as quickly as it had begun, as teen love—built on scorching but shifting sands—so often does. Ensnared in the stepped-up swirl of activity that greeted us at U-E, we were like goldfish tossed into the ocean. The "playing field" had changed. Our paths did not cross all the time anymore. Our circle of acquaintances mutated.

Confronted by this altered landscape, Laurene and I were not sure how to react. Little disagreements between us mushroomed into full-blown arguments. Resentments escalated into jealousies. The fluctuating conditions that accompany adolescence brought strange new forces to bear on our relationship.

And then it was over. "Breaking up is hard to do" had never carried such meaning; my heart had never been filled with such ache.

Autumn's other routines continued. They took place exactly as I'd become used to seeing them unfold.

Grampa Lee brought home sawdust he had swept up and bagged at my uncle's mill and watched, his eyes probing for the slightest sign of a misappropriation of material, as I spread it evenly around the roots of his rose bushes. If the only sound I heard during this ritual was the spat of tobacco juice cascading in a brownish-yellow stream toward the driveway, I knew I'd performed the task to his exacting specifications.

Grampa Blossom threw an extra log on the fire when we arrived in Apalachin after church for Sunday dinner. While my grandmother and mother prepared a lavish meal—often embellished with gravy gleaned from the fat of a roast, and my grandmother's homemade bread (hot to the touch)—the men retired to the living room to talk construction or to mull the fortunes of the New York Football Giants. The Giants—Y.A. Tittle, Pat Summerall, Frank Gifford, Roosevelt Grier, Alex Webster, Andy Robistelli, Sam Huff and the other names and faces I was so familiar with— would have the Eagles or Browns or Colts or Redskins in their pocket that afternoon merely by setting foot on the turf at Yankee Stadium, the men agreed.

The bald-headed Tittle, the Giants' aging quarterback—who often played bloodied but unbowed, slinging the ball overhand or sidearm as an opponent sent him sprawling onto his derriere—was my favorite player.

As an impressionable kid, I admired guys who could "take a licking and keep on ticking"—just like Timex watches, whose durability was trumpeted through the use of that phrase by John Cameron Swayze in popular television commercials he did for the company. Across the Southern Tier, I had seldom seen any high school football player play tougher than U-E's own Ronnie Macon. I derived enormous satisfaction out of watching Macon— a veritable string bean, who weighed maybe one hundred fifteen pounds, soaking wet—fearlessly attack onrushing runners from his linebacker spot. Macon didn't back up for anyone. Ronnie Macon, Dick Streno and Bobby Atkinson were three of the small guys who would play tough for Fran Angeline in the years I was at U-E. In the pros, Y.A. Tittle was the same way. He took his hits, picked himself off the ground and came right back at you.

Over our food, my grandmother would launch into a long prayer in her high-pitched voice, thanking God for our countless blessings and beseeching Him to rid the earth of evildoers and satanic influences. Although she never mentioned him by name, my grandmother, I surmised, certainly considered my Uncle George—who was married to my Aunt Peg (Margaret Hallberg)— to be a card-carrying member of the devil's rank and file, because of his penchant for drinking, smoking and generally unholy behavior. With her typical enthusiasm as a Bible-brandishing crusader for Christ, my grandmother was always trying to save Uncle George from a certain trip to the burning bowels of Hell, and she would lecture him incessantly about his many faults. "It's never too late to take the Lord into your heart. Repent now!" she'd say. She maintained a steady drumbeat of criticism, tempered with doses of encouragement, in an attempt to turn Uncle George around. To no avail, however.

As I sat with my fingers interlocked respectfully in front of me while my grandmother prayed, I marveled at her capacity to produce a fresh litany each and every time. She accomplished this with no prepared notes or noticeable advance effort, and rendered the long-winded benediction flawlessly. I asked her about it once. She told me, "anyone can pray if they have God in their heart."

She offered the same explanation for her hymn singing, which would raise the rafters. "You don't need any voice training to sing triumphantly like I do," she'd say. "It's God's spirit at work."

I wished—but never said as much to my grandmother—that her prayers would include fewer references to the devil and his debilitating effects on society and more requests for God to give the Giants the wherewithal they'd need to win on Sunday. "Just once," I whispered to myself, "I wish she'd ask God to let Frank Gifford break a long one or to help Sam Huff drop Cleveland's Jim Brown in his tracks behind the line of scrimmage."

She never did, though.

My grandparent Blossoms' home in the country had captured my fancy since I was young. It wasn't an E-J house, like my grandparent Lees' place, but rather a home they had mostly stitched together themselves. It sat back about a hundred yards on an unpaved road, was accessed by a long dirt driveway and was bordered to the rear and on one side by deep woods. The woods, thick and moist and stretching seemingly to infinity, provided my brothers and I with a natural habitat for a playground. We built tree huts with discarded boards my grandfather gave us and hung out in these dwellings, high above the bed of the forest. We hunted for rabbits and squirrels with small makeshift bows and arrows and slingshots. We copped rides in a homemade buggy my Uncle Jim (my mother's brother and my grandparents' youngest child) had constructed out of scrap metal, old tires and an old gasoline engine. We played softball in the front yard. We took naps in the shade of an old pine tree at the edge of the woods. When I got older I stayed at my grandparents' house often on weekends; exhausted from a day's dredging of the woods for thrills, I would drift into a deep sleep to the sounds of crickets chirping in the yard and remain in a blissful slumber until awakened by the scent of bacon sizzling on the stove. Breakfast was served!

My grandparents' home became another of the many places I loved to visit as a boy. The list had grown quite large. By the age of fourteen it included several newly discovered spots. Most of these were in and around Endicott, which brimmed with attractions a boy could sink his teeth into.

One of these was Tri-Cities Airport on Route 17C on the way out of town, heading west from Endicott toward Campville. My first visit to Tri-Cities Airport had come on August 27th, 1956, when I was ten and my parents took my brothers and me to an air show and rodeo that were being held in conjunction with the village of Endicott's fifty-sixth anniversary celebration.

Tri-Cities Airport provided me with my first glimpse of daring men in their flying machines. It served privately owned aircraft. Small piper cubs would swoop low over the Susquehanna River and taxi to a stop in front of the airfield's small hangar.

By October of 1960 I had already witnessed a lot of U-E football and basketball games and had the memories to show for it. I had also become such an avid follower of the Tigers that I fumed along with the rest of the faithful when the team sank into stagnation, in the mid-1950's—culminating with a horrendous campaign in 1959 under the irrepressible but ineffectual Nick DiNunzio.

DiNunzio, like "Ty" Cobb, had been at U-E for a long time—since 1941. He would stay on until 1978. During his career at U-E, he demonstrated his versatility as a mentor to athletes by coaching several sports. He also started the golf team. His one year as varsity football coach—in 1959—was a washout, however.

Now it was Fran Angeline's turn, and hopes for a rebirth were soaring. Angeline wasted no time implementing change from top to bottom. The concrete stands on the north side of the stadium soon became U-E's home side; we were no longer relegated to the wooden bleachers on the far side, which held far fewer spectators and which were in a state of disconnect from the school and grounds. Saturday-night home games were introduced too, giving U-E sole possession of the evening, among area schools, for its games. Saturday night was "good for fightin'," Elton John would assert. It was certainly good enough for U-E football.

Despite the loss to JC the week before, optimism prevailed on the eve of the first home game of the Angeline era, against Ithaca on Saturday, October 8th. The charged atmosphere Angeline had already kindled could be seen in the chatter taking place in Henry's (a tobacco store at the corner of Washington Avenue and North Street), at Giordano's (a barber shop on North Street), at Tedeschi's Market (on Odell Avenue on the North Side), at Shapiro's and Kline's (men's clothing stores on The Avenue), in the office of Mayor E. Raymond Lee (no relation to my family) and among Endicott's cops and firefighters.

Our optimism proved to be well founded. In their most inspired performance for Angeline to that point, the Tigers exploded for two touchdowns in the second quarter.

Heightened anticipation prevailed from the outset. On the side-lines, as U-E and Ithaca players waited for the whistle signaling it was time for the kickoff, I could see the squat figure of John Julian bouncing up and down as if he were a marionette. U-E fans adored Julian; to see the short, plump John Julian this animated and pumped up sent shivers of glee through the crowd. The younger players seemed to be filled with pride and purpose too: amid the jostling and yelling, Bobby Atkinson and Bill Pickering and Jim Michael raced back and forth, battering helmets with the player next to them like goats locking horns.

The student body's enthusiasm for the encounter as the start of action neared evolved into near hysteria, gripping even usually reserved classmates of mine like Fred Cosin, Dave Best, Bob

Smith, Anne Wahila and Gil Norton. These five were gifted scholars whose flirtations with exhibitionism normally amounted to nothing more disruptive than a sigh of satisfaction when one of their papers came back with a "99" or "100" scribbled across the top of the page. I had grown up with Dave Best in West Corners; the good breeding that had been inculcated in him and his brothers and sisters by their IBM'er dad and their mother never failed to impress acquaintances. Cosin, Smith, Wahila and Norton exhibited similar academic correctness. I took a lukewarm approach to my studies; they were serious students. They rose rapidly to the top of the class, like cream to the surface of a bottle of milk from Magic City Ice Co.

This night their minds were on football.

It didn't take long for Bobby Colburn and Co. to assert their superiority, or for a loud groundswell of approval to explode among U-E fans. The din that filled Ty Cobb Stadium that night would become commonplace in the years to follow. As U-E football settled into its Saturday-night routine, people took notice. From then on, the specter of the field lights beaming at the edge of Endicott would be all the indication motorists—traveling east and west on Route 17, just across the river—needed to know that it was show time in Endicott.

I had become accustomed to hearing about the country's high school football hotbeds: the plains communities of Texas; the coal towns of Pennsylvania; the tidewater towns of Virginia. Along the banks of the Susquehanna River in the autumn of 1960, a similar phenomenon was taking shape, as U-E football re-emerged.

Under Fran Angeline, U-E would resemble a human tank; Endicotters would come to know that when the sixth day of the week arrived and the sun sank low, it was time to inch toward the portals of Ty Cobb Stadium. U-E fans would become another weapon in the Tigers' arsenal. Several thousand strong, they would summon forth from their lungs and throats a mighty rumble that planted the seeds of doubt in opposing teams' minds even before the referee for the night—Bill Starring, Bob Harter or Steve Charsky, perhaps—blew the whistle to start play.

Over time, Angeline's teams would achieve on the gridiron the same sort of success the village had become used to seeing from the hands of pre-eminent homegrown or adopted sons like George F. Johnson, Thomas J. Watson Sr., cartoonist Johnny Hart, Shortstop Johnny Logan, Major League Umpire Ron Luciano and Professional Golfer Richie Karl.

On Saturday nights during the Angeline years, Ty Cobb Stadium became the Roman Coliseum, and U-E opponents were fed to the Tigers. Week after week, year after year, Angeline-coached teams gave Endicott a reason to believe.

The players who wore the Orange and Black arrived and moved through the program in a steady stream. Many of them blazed into view for the briefest of moments: sometimes for only a season, sometimes for only a single game, or a series of downs or a single play, before fading away, their names and faces lingering on the consciousness long after they had drifted into military or civilian life.

Against Ithaca High's "Little Red" that night, it was Bobby Colburn's turn to break out. Colburn was in certain regards the unlikeliest of candidates to produce the kind of performance he mustered that evening. As a transfer from Vestal, he'd been in the U-E system for only a year. At Vestal, as a seventh and eighth grader, he'd shown promise as both a back and a lineman, but then had missed his entire frosh campaign after breaking a leg in three places. His football career seemed to be in jeopardy. Fortunately for U-E, he was back, stronger than ever.

The Bobby Colburn who had finally surfaced in the JC game the week before now stuck it to the Little Red and their coach, Joe Moresco. By the time the Tigers, exhausted but exultant, trotted toward their clubhouse at the eastern end of the stadium, Colburn had amassed 220 yards and two touchdowns in a 26-6 rout. He'd been a gale-force factor, carrying the pigskin seven times from scrimmage for one hundred yards, posting ninety-two yards on four punt returns, returning a kickoff for nineteen yards, catching a ten-yard pass from Dave Sammon and picking up four yards on an intercepted lateral! That last play had set up a U-E touchdown.

Bobby Colburn's two biggest moves left me dazzled and spent from shouting. Gathering in an Ithaca punt in the second quarter, he headed straight up the gut, veered right at about midfield and steamed down the sidelines. It went on the board as a seventy five-yard TD. Hardly having caught his breath, he then intercepted a pass thrown by Ithaca's Mel Robinson and, although seemingly stopped twice, tore into the end zone from forty-seven yards out.

The victory was the second of Angeline's budding U-E coaching career and the Tigers' most impressive showing to date. I had no doubt that many more victories would follow.

Vestal's Dick Hoover, Angeline's next foe, seemed impressed. "Right now, they're as good as any team in the conference," Hoover told the newspaper. He expressed concern about U-E's "quick line and versatile backfield."

The Tigers' resounding triumph triggered a week's worth of nonstop talk throughout the village; this began on Sunday morning as parishioners gathered outside St. Anthony's and St. Peter and Paul's churches on the North Side and in other houses of worship. It continued unabated on Monday, Tuesday and Wednesday within the ranks of newly appointed Chief of Police Delbert Pemberton's department, among Fire Chief Paul L. Brown and his men at the Central fire house and up and down Washington Avenue. People could not enter the main post office at the corner of Washington Avenue and Broad Street without collaring Postmaster Raymond Delaney or a mail clerk or a mail carrier in order to render their assessment of the Tigers' superb effort. In the hallways, classrooms and offices of U-E High School, "Tiger talk" even pushed discussions of Shakespeare to the side in Dennis Bottino's College Preparatory (CP) English class: a rare circumstance. Other teachers—Bob Barno (History), Carl Zonio (French), Ed Goodnow (Math), Joe Kazlauskas (Science)—cheerfully entered into the dialogue about U-E's revived football prospects, or at least tolerated the inevitable digressions into what could be expected next from our suddenly ferocious Tigers.

U-E's football program, a travesty of late, was a joke no more. Pride ran particularly strong in the village's heavily Italian, Roman Catholic community. Endicott's Catholics had always been appreciative of the contributions of pioneers like George F. Johnson; Johnson had even donated a residence he owned behind St. Ambrose Church on Washington Avenue to the church for a rectory. Johnson had also assisted hugely (and without even being asked) in the completion of St. Joseph's Church, at Hayes Avenue and Witherall Street. St Joe's was a showpiece of the village's Slovak populace. Riding past the site one afternoon in 1929, Johnson had spotted members of the congregation helping their pastor, the Rev. Florian C. Billy, who was dressed in coveralls, finish the job. When he returned the next morning for another look at the Gothic brownstone edifice taking shape, Johnson, impressed, vowed to match, dollar for dollar, money raised for the project. Several weeks later, Johnson presented church officials with a check for $28,000—equaling the amount that had been pledged. After the church, one of the largest in Endicott at the time, was finished, Johnson gave the congregation a new organ.

Angeline, by returning to his hometown and his alma mater, and by imbuing the school and the village with fresh vigor, quickly cemented his status as a worthy successor to men like Henry B. Endicott and George F. Johnson.

Like them, Angeline burned with ambition. Like them, he appreciated the village's illustrious history as a factory town. Like them, he yearned to make his mark and to boost Endicott's stature once again.

Across the river that week, the team that represented the next hurdle in U-E's path was practicing under the observant eye of a canny coach whose yen to win matched Angeline's: Richard "Dick" Hoover.

On our side of the Susquehanna, the Tigers got ready for their stiffest test yet. Games between U-E and Vestal would become known within just a few years as "The Rivalry": as fierce a battle of wills as any mounted between man and monster, man and man, school and school, nation and nation. Their jarring collisions would result in the largest crowds ever to gather for high school football in the Triple Cities. The games would produce some of the greatest football the area would ever witness.

The stage was set for U-E vs. the Vestal Golden Bears of the Angeline-Hoover years, Act I.

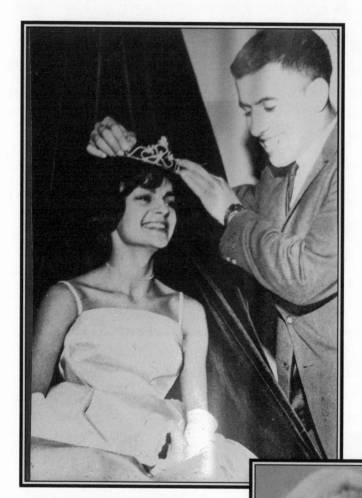

Above: Jeanne Randesi, the prettiest girl on campus, being crowned Homecoming Queen by football player Ken Pacioni.

To right: Pat Dibler; the definition of the word voluptuous at U-E High School in the early 1960's.

A RIVALRY CATCHES FIRE

By the age of fourteen I had added the word voluptuous to my vocabulary. There was no need to consult Webster's on its meaning. One look at Patricia Dibler, a classmate, was enough to arouse sexual urges of the sort that linger around the loins, teasing and taunting, and deflecting the mind from important business. Not even football stood a chance against the pull exerted by a girl of Pat Dibler's caliber.

There were at Union-Endicott High School in October of 1960 a number of girls who could be considered femme fatales. Penny Chetko, who lived in West Endicott and who ran with the Perfetti crowd, drew admiring glances everywhere she went. Chetko was tall and slender and possessed long, ravishing black hair and a pretty face to go with an engaging personality. We'd become friends at Jennie F. Snapp, where Chetko was an honor student and where she and Pat Steenburg—like Laurene Perfetti and I—had fallen into a steamy relationship. Though demure and a little shy, Penny radiated wholesomeness and was fun to be around.

Josephine Shady, a neighbor of Perfetti's on Wilma Street, was small but buxom, and her freckled cheeks, dancing eyes and merry demeanor made her a favorite.

Back in elementary school, when the first stirrings of want struck, I found myself playing Spin the Bottle with Patty Witter, who also lived in West Corners, in my garage when my parents were not around, and savoring the sweetness of her kiss on my lips.

In all of Endicott and certainly among members of the U-E Class of '63, there was no more coveted a catch than Jeanne Randesi. Randesi, small and pert, oozed vivaciousness and vitality. She was as friendly as they come. Randesi treated everyone—long-time cronies and new acquaintances alike—the same. These qualities magnified her stunning natural beauty. She was a knockout from head to toe. A discerning talent scout prowling the streets of New York City, Genoa or Venice for a new sensation to grace the pages of a teenage modeling magazine could not have found a more photogenic candidate than Jeanne Randesi. She appeared to me to be an amalgamation of the best attributes of the celluloid stars of the day; she had Sophia Loren's smoldering allure, Gina Lollibridga's curves, Doris Day's innocent playful nature and Natalie Wood's mysteriousness. Jeanne Randesi was a perfect "10" long before actress Bo Derek established that number as the one by which males would forever quantify a female's sexual appeal.

Boys attending U-E in the early 60's envied Bobby Atkinson for his athletic abilities, which translated into letterman status in all of the school's three major sports; they envied him just as much for his role as Jeanne Randesi's steady.

It did not surprise me that Jeanne Randesi and Pat Dibler both became cheerleaders at Union-Endicott, or that Randesi earned the title of Homecoming Queen our senior year.

Dibler, blond and statuesque, seemed oblivious to the assets with which she'd been endowed. If that was the case, she was alone in this regard. The very sight of Dibler ambling, Marilyn Monroe-like, into Mr. Turver's biology class in a blouse or a tight-knit sweater, her "points" situated "firm and high" as Bob Seger would put it in his song "Night Moves," was enough to cause the males in the room to push aside their contemplations of dissec-

tions and dream instead of torrid afternoon dalliances with her—
far from public view.

These distractions notwithstanding, Union-Endicott's game at
Vestal was grabbing a lion's share of the attention in school and
in the press as the week progressed. No one could have predicted,
as the Tigers ran through their preparatory drills on our side of the
Susquehanna, and the Bears did the same on the Vestal side, that
a rivalry of monstrous proportions was in the making.

In the years to follow, the battle for bragging rights between the
two schools would be imbued with all of the ingredients one
would expect to find in an ongoing, unsettled struggle-to-the-
death of superpowers: intrigue; suspense; chicanery; bluster; sub-
terfuge. The annual meeting of U-E and Vestal would become
much more than a skirmish for high school football superiority,
played out before overflow crowds (these throngs would pack the
bleachers and ring the fields ten and fifteen rows deep; they would
watch from the top of the respective press boxes and from the
small knoll behind the visitors' side at Vestal and from windows
at U-E in the back of the school overlooking the field).

In a larger sense U-E vs. Vestal was a test of wills between two
very different but equally proud communities: Endicott, a factory
town, and Vestal, a rural community sprinkled with meadows and
farms. It would also become a chess match between two coaches—
U-E's fiery Fran Angeline and Vestal's reserved Dick Hoover—
who were almost exact opposites in many ways and whose respective personalities served to inflame the masses even more. It
would become a game that would affect the very fiber of life in
both communities. Fittingly, it would be shifted to early
November—the last game of the season on both schools' schedules—so that when all other issues had been resolved the only
thing that still mattered was Endicott vs. Vestal.

It made no difference how poorly or magnificently either team had performed until then. When they met, everything was on the line.

The week of the '60 game, Vestal players with names Endicotters already knew well from the sports pages—Schultz and Kaminsky and Cordi and Fenstemacher and Gillard and Throup—rode brazenly up and down East Main Street and Washington Avenue in Endicott in their cars. Green and gold colors flapped in the wind. The Vestal players' voices shouted challenges or defiance. Endicotters returned fire just as vociferously. Neither camp was afraid to venture into the other's territory. In homes in the evening, in barrooms like the Vestal Inn in Vestal, in restaurants like Augie's in Union, at shops like Howard's Florist in Vestal and Esther Immerman on The Avenue and Westbrook's in Union, the conversation transcended the merits of the two teams; references were made to the assets of Endicott versus the assets of Vestal. It was not uncommon during the course of such debate, as the years and the legendary collisions ensued, for Endicotters to invoke the name of Pat Mitchell, whose homemade ice cream, dipped from canisters in a parlor not far from the bridge connecting Endicott and Vestal, drew customers from both sides of the river. Vestalites would counter with a reference to their own Carvel ice-cream store.

On and on the comparisons went.

"The Game" almost always lived up to the hype. Typical were the meetings of the early 60's when the rivalry was just starting to materialize, and especially the match-up of '64: the swan song for the finest player ever to don Vestal colors—Bobby Campbell. The records coming into the game: U-E 7-0-0, Vestal 6-0-1.

The outcome: a 13-13 tie!

The coaches became the focal point of the rivalry.

Hoover, the older of the two, was the personification of mellowness. He deftly and cordially answered sportswriters' questions as the scribes probed for clues to the Bears' state of mind or inklings of Vestal's game plan. Hoover projected a fatherly image in practice and on the sidelines, allowing his more tightly wound lieutenants—men like Frank Buran—to rake a player for a timid block or to berate an official for a questionable call. Hoover was content to nod or wink or smile by way of registering his affirmation. Pacing in front of the Vestal bench in black football cleats, a tan trench coat and a short-brimmed hat atop his head, and with a game program, rolled up, in his left hand, Hoover appeared to be the picture of calm and steadfast generalship. His impassive expression mirrored Vestal's methodical, businesslike approach to blocking and tackling and running. Hoover operated in an atmosphere of utter restraint, seldom revealing such emotions as anxiousness or jubilation, whether his team was up or down. Pandemonium could be breaking out all around him; his imperturbability seldom faltered. His and the persona the town of Vestal projected were one and the same: nothing fancy, ma'am, just results.

The image Angeline fostered couldn't have offered a starker contrast. As the heir apparent in the eyes of residents of Endicott to luminaries like George F. Johnson and Thomas J. Watson Sr., Angeline had a legacy of extraordinary feats to uphold, and he attacked the challenge with a relentless determination. In short order he established himself as Endicott's next galactic presence. No one—not even Dick Hoover of Vestal—was going to keep him from accomplishing his mission.

Where Hoover was agreeable, Angeline was abrasive. Where Hoover was accommodating, Angeline was confrontational. Where Hoover was laid back, Angeline was in-your-face. Where Hoover was slow to boil, Angeline was quick-tempered. Where Hoover was patient, Angeline was driven by a sense of urgency. Where Hoover seemingly did not fret about the small stuff, Angeline worried about every little thing, right down to the minutest detail.

As the U-E vs. Vestal game approached, the temperature rose between the two schools. The coaches sensed this. The players sensed it. The assistant coaches sensed it. The media sensed it. The fans sensed it.

The conflicting approaches the two took were reflected even in their different offensive gambits. Hoover relied heavily on what came to be known as Vestal's short punt attack, involving an animated shift of the Bears' ends and backs just before the snap of the ball. This ploy invariably suckered the other team in, resulting in an offside call. It used to infuriate me, sitting in the stands, knowing that Vestal was going to pull that crap—and get away with it. Angeline protested the Vestal short punt as an illegal tactic, to no avail. U-E, meanwhile, trotted out its hurry-up, or racehorse, game, and later its triple option and Top Gun ruses. These too brought cries of foul from foes.

The 1960 game drew what the media dubbed a "banner crowd"—the kind of assemblage that would become a staple backdrop to the yearly battle. The bleachers of Ty Cobb Stadium were awash in Orange and Black and Green and Gold. Wandering the east end zone with Bill Thayer, Bobby Muir, Kevin Plugh, Carl Letson and John Watts, I kept a wary eye on Vestal's big guns stretching themselves into readiness on the visitors side of the field: Hoover's son, Glenn Hoover; Bill Montross, a running back with a knack for slithering out of defenders' grasps; Tony Lenkiewicz; Al Anderson; and Dan Murphy, a gangly, six-foot seven-inch pass receiver.

I would have said "no way" if someone had suggested to me, that day, that I would later become friends with Dan Murphy, or that "Murph" and I would decide on the spur of the moment in the winter of '64-'65 to leave the employ of IBM and our factory jobs on North Street in Endicott and take off for California. Preposterous as the notion of a collaboration of the sort was in October of 1960, when Dan Murphy and Vestal were archenemies, it came to pass a little over four years later. A strange twist indeed!

Murph and I were accompanied on our trip by my Uncle Bun, who tagged along so that he too could play golf en route to paying a visit to his brother "Red" Turner in San Jose. Together, Murphy, my uncle and I followed legendary Route 66 across the Southwest, stopping to eat steak in Oklahoma City and Amarillo, to talk our way onto a private golf course in Phoenix (The Wigwam) and to shoot craps on "The Strip" in Las Vegas. After depositing my uncle in northern California, Murph and I headed down the coast toward Los Angeles. We were compelled by the notion of landing exciting new jobs and meeting skimpily-clad "California girls" on the beach. We ended up selling Rainbow vacuum cleaners door to door. Then Murph received his military draft notice—ordering him back to Syracuse for a pre-induction physical. Disillusioned with the Golden State and homesick, we headed east again. Our taste of California had lasted all of three months.

Knowing the talents Murphy and the rest of the Bears brought to the 1960 U-E vs. Vestal game, I sensed that the Tigers would have to come out smoking to beat Dick Hoover's team. And they did. Facing an early 7-0 deficit, the Tigers began to march. On the sixth play of an early thrust toward the Vestal goal line, Dave Sammon and Dick Pugh hooked up on a sixteen-yard touchdown pass. Ed Ciotoli kicked the extra point. U-E had neutralized Vestal's initial strike to square the score at 7-7.

U-E fans have never experienced loftier highs, or deeper lows, than when the Tigers face Vestal. In that first meeting between an Angeline-led U-E team and a Hoover-coached Vestal squad, lows were in abundance in the second half as the Bears, employing their fiendishly deceptive short-punt formation, the "T" and even some single wing, tallied twice more to win, 20-7.

In the years to follow the season-ending match-up would be nicknamed "The Rivalry" or "The Championship of the River." It would pit great football teams in all-out war before upwards of twenty thousand fans every November, and it would involve the inevitable comparisons on other fronts as well: Pat Mitchell's Ice Cream vs. Carvel; Grover's Pig Stand vs. A&W Root Beer; Don Owen Pontiac vs. Ken Wilson Chevrolet; Washington Avenue vs. Front Street; and the Strand and Lyric theaters vs. the Vestal Drive-In. In all regards, in my estimation, Endicott had it all over Vestal. I wanted it to be the same on the football field, each and every time.

Through the ups and downs that would transpire in the Vestal series and against other teams U-E faced, I never lost faith in Angeline. Others did, however. Some U-E fans even turned their disgust into boos. This happened about midway through the '69 season when U-E, a heavy favorite in a first-ever meeting with Chenango Valley High School, played atrociously. The Tigers racked up more than one hundred yards in penalties. Even though they were knocking on the door at the end, they lost the game, 6-0. That night, some obviously disgruntled fans snuck into Angeline's garage and lathered the family station wagon with what Angeline later described as "a mixture of flour, eggs, ketchup and karo syrup."

The weekend of that CV game represented one of the low points in Angeline's career. It epitomized what he himself referred to as "the U-E football roller coaster" of the late 60's. On the eve of the 1969 Vestal game, a few weeks later, the Angeline children's classmates called the coach a bum. Not-so-subtle hints filtered through the village that he should quit, or be fired. With such epithets ringing in his ears, Angeline took U-E across the Susquehanna to confront Vestal. The Bears came into the game with a 6-1-1 record. Angeline's neck was in the noose. But, lifted by "one of the most perfect, inspirational performances by any of our squads...," as he put it, that U-E team, led by QB/Safety Tom Mason and Defensive End and Captain Monte Cole, destroyed the Bears, 32-14.

The '69 win over Vestal represented one of many high points Angeline would experience before retiring in '93.

The '60 game would not be one of them.

The '60 game did serve to establish my sophomore classmate, hard-nosed halfback Bobby Atkinson, as a comer. Atkinson teamed up with junior fullback Bill Pickering to give U-E fans something to cheer about that day. Two unlikelier bedfellows could not have been found than Atkinson and Pickering. "Atky" was a tough customer. He was not big on social graces. He possessed the sculpted body of a warrior. In school, he oozed the aura of the athlete even while walking down the hall in street clothes, with books under his arm. He was not afraid to let his uncouth side show. He'd blow farts for the fun of it. In "the Pit" (U-E's basketball gymnasium), he would sometimes discreetly deliver a forearm shiver to an opponent as they manueverued for position underneath the balcony's overhang, if the officials weren't paying attention. Off the field, Pickering was more of a gentleman than Bobby Atkinson; also, Pickering was baby-faced and bore a trace of portliness around the hips. On the field, though, "No. 39" could chug with the best of them as he carried the ball on short bursts through the defensive line.

I now wondered, as I settled into the routine of high-school life, if Atkinson and Pickering could lift the Tigers out of their funk as the team got ready for back-to-back games on the road: at Elmira Southside and Utica Proctor.

Or was the loss to Vestal the start of a horrendous, irreversible slide?

Bill Pickering; No. 39 for the Tigers, chugging for short yardage in a 1962 game.

STUNG BY THE GREEN HORNETS

Nothing was more important to my grandfather and my dad and his brothers than automobiles. Trading, or "swapping," cars every year or so had become a pastime with them, as hunting and fishing were with other men. On Saturdays, individually and sometimes in groups of two or three, they would scour the local car lots from one end of Endicott to another in search of the set of wheels that was the sharpest and most efficient to be found. Often they would head straight for a car that had caught their eye as they traveled back and forth from job sites during the week, in which case a picture of it would be imbedded in their brain, reminding them that a closer inspection, and a test drive, were only days or hours away.

In Endicott in 1960 there was no shortage of car dealerships from which to choose. I often accompanied my father as he made the rounds of the different lots: Don Owen Pontiac; Endicott Rambler; Gault Chevrolet; Alderman's; Newing Motors; Valley Motors; Endicott Sales; Earl Hendrick's. Occasionally he would venture across the river to Vestal to check out the cars at lots like Henry Carroll's, on the Vestal Parkway, lured there, for instance, by an advertisement he'd seen in the newspaper for "the new

Morris '1000'...your BIGGEST small-car buy." The ad described the Morris '1000' as a two-door sedan that could comfortably seat five people and that boasted an attractive chrome grill and whitewall tires; all of this, the ad said, plus the promise of "over forty miles per gallon," for $1495. The Morris was too small, though. My father liked big, roomy cars. They had to have no less than eight cylinders, too.

My father was not a mechanical guy but he considered himself to be an astute judge of an automobile's character. He was knowledgeable about all of the models on the market: past and present. He sized up cars the way a man sizes up a woman, ever on the lookout for disqualifying flaws. The doors had to "thwack" shut solidly, the motor had to purr, the interior had to smell clean. Rust, however inconspicuous, generated an instantaneous thumbs-down. He also knew what was out there. When I was thirteen and starting to get interested in cars, I asked him about a 1958 Impala convertible that was for sale. "That was Bill Gault's personal car," he said, referring to the owner of Gault Chevrolet. "V8, turbo glide, power steering, power brakes, air, radio, heater. A beauty, but they're asking way too much at $2995."

My dad had a keen eye for superior cars and could not wait for the end of the week so that he could lay aside his carpenter's apron and chalk line in order to spend a few hours examining a 1955 four-door Nash Ambassador at Endicott Sales, a Ford Falcon at Newing Motors, a 1958 Plymouth Custom suburban four-door (with automatic transmission, radio, heater, whitewall tires and a red and ivory finish...$1895) at Alderman's or a red '57 Mercury hardtop coupe selling for $1495 at Endicott Lincoln-Mercury.

I learned to drive on a sleek green Mercury my dad owned and loved. The shift was on the column. The car whispered as it moved down the road. I couldn't get the hang of coordinating the clutch pedal and hand action that was required, however. When I was at the wheel, it would lurch ahead in fits and starts as my father, trying to contain his exasperation, watched nervously from

RODNEY LEE ◆ 149

the passenger seat, ready to jump at any moment if his intervention became necessary.

My grandfather, my uncles and my dad were all masters of the art of barter. Theirs were familiar faces to the car dealers on Nanticoke Avenue in West Endicott and on North Street and East Main Street in Endicott. It was a given when they walked onto the lot that serious negotiation was about to take place. All of the Lee men had apparently inherited from my grandfather the uncanny knack of turning the most innocuous nick on a bumper or fender, the tiniest smudge on a tire, the smallest blemish on a hood or the slightest squeak in a door into a demand that the dealer shave a couple of hundred dollars off the sticker price. Many times after my dad and I took a spin in a Desoto or a Packard, I'd listen as he described to a salesperson the nature of a particular problem: a "shimmy" in the front end; the telltale throaty cough of a muffler going bad; the distinctive "rattle" that suggested a screw had become dislodged in the dashboard. Any of these conditions were grounds for the infliction of a severe tongue-lashing on the dealer, or one of his henchmen, when we returned to the lot, in an attempt to force them to agree to take corrective measures at no charge, or to drop the price substantially.

The Lee men had gotten this routine down to a science. They were even capable of manufacturing all sorts of "problems" that needed to be addressed. Picayune complaints of this nature always helped their bargaining position; a grumpy attitude didn't hurt, either. No one was better at putting on his game face than my grandfather, whose smile and laugh would give way to a scowl the instant he arrived at a car dealership.

Not being taken to the cleaners by a car dealer was a matter of pride in the Lee family. My grandfather and his sons would settle for nothing but success on this front; it was the thrill of the give and take as much as having grown disenchanted with their present vehicle that inspired them to trade every spring, or every couple of years. They dealt almost exclusively in used cars; my mother can remember my dad owning a new car only once: a green and white Packard that he drove home straight out of the showroom. "And we had nothing but trouble with that car!" she said.

Although I did not share my father's fascination with automobiles, I did appreciate the "little dust coupe" that my friend Bill Thayer began tooling around in soon after acquiring his driver's license. The car impressed me almost as much as the extensive and precisely arranged workshop that Bill's father had set up in the basement of their home in Glendale. Bill and I celebrated Bill's newfound mobility by taking off to points north one afternoon after school. We came to rest in front of a diner in Marathon, near Whitney Point. There, to the sounds of Cokes slurped through a straw and Little Richard's voice blasting out the vocals to "Good Golly, Miss Molly" over the radio, we dreamed big.

Bill Thayer had by this time become a regular companion, joining those I had grown up with in West Corners who had moved through West Corners Elementary and Jennie F. Snapp with me: Tom Giordano; Bobby Muir; Chuck Mitchell; Mike Stone; the Crawford brothers; Al Rossi; Dave Brewer; Ken Crump; Dave Best; Tom Morris; Kevin Cahill; George Mathyas.

Thayer, curly-haired, articulate and erudite, was a more serious student than me. In high school, he relished extended, involved discussions—especially those involving world history and politics. He took copious notes in a stilted backhand. Though our personalities were different, we clicked.

Cars—big, dazzling, colorful boats with leather seats, black dice hanging from the rear-view mirror, lots of chrome, whitewall tires, loud mufflers and a radio that boomed across the countryside—were beginning to attract my attention. Before long, I figured, I would have one of my own and be able to deck it out in Orange and Black streamers for the ride with my buddies to home and away games.

The thought of the upcoming Saturday's game against Elmira Southside prompted a shudder of apprehension. The odds did not favor U-E. The dismal second-half showing against Vestal still festered like an open sore, for one thing. Besides which, ESS was coming into the game with one of its better squads; indeed, the Green Hornets hadn't lost yet. To make matters worse, we had to play on their turf, at Parker Field in Elmira—an environment that dripped with venom whenever opposing teams came to town.

The city of Elmira, situated on the Chemung River near the border with Pennsylvania, about an hour west of Endicott, had a reputation as a rough place. Fights at U-E-ESS games were not uncommon. I often wondered what Mark Twain, who spent summers in Elmira, at Quarry Farm, from 1870 to 1903, writing portions of *Tom Sawyer*, *Huckleberry Finn* and *Life on the Mississippi*, among other works, found so endearing about the city. Going from Endicott's tame streets to Elmira's hardscrabble, uninviting downtown felt like walking into Dodge City. Imagine my surprise when, years later, I learned that Elmira had been ranked 37th among "Best Smaller Places" by *Forbes* magazine (in May of 2000).

Today, Elmira bills itself as "the soaring capital of America" but one of its greatest claims to fame was a young man who kept his feet very much on the ground: Ernie Davis. Davis, "The Elmira Express," was a gifted running back who won the Heisman Trophy as college football's premier player at Syracuse University after a brilliant scholastic career at Elmira Free Academy (EFA was the other Elmira school U-E played). Davis died of leukemia before getting a chance to suit up for Coach Paul Brown's Cleveland Browns of the National Football League (NFL).

As an individual of strong moral character, Ernie Davis left an indelible impression on those with whom he came into contact— including one of Coach Angeline's early-60's U-E squads. Amazingly, the ever-so-brief encounter between Ernie Davis and that Tiger team took place *off* the field: in the visiting team's locker room at EFA. It was so unusual an occurrence that the young U-E players on the receiving end of the gesture must have been tempted to pinch themselves when they reached adulthood, as people are prone to do in such circumstances, by way of reassurance that something so extraordinary had really happened.

Back in his hometown for a few days, Davis made an unannounced appearance in the U-E locker room just before game time to welcome the Tigers. He offered a few remarks on his love of the sport. Then he was gone. "I shall never forget this young man…" Angeline wrote in his autobiography, *This Tiger's Tale*, published in 1996. Maybe, I surmised later, Angeline had seen in Davis many of the qualities he would exhibit throughout his own life as a player, teacher and coach: certitude; decency; forthrightness; loyalty; an unwavering commitment to excellence. Maybe that's why Davis' poignant address to a U-E team moved Angeline so deeply.

My school in 1960, like my village in 1906, was embarking on an odyssey of discovery and accomplishment. This time it was on the football field. In the years to follow, Coach Angeline would earn a spot for himself in the pantheon of luminaries Endicott could claim as having been instrumental in shaping its destiny. George F. Johnson and Henry B. Endicott and Thomas J. Watson Sr. topped the list, of course. But there had been others:

- Dudley S. Mercereau, the colorful long-time clerk in the Town of Union, whose ashes were scattered over Round Hill after he died in January of 1944.

- Wendall Soltis, the first member of the ethnic community to become mayor of Endicott (in 1979).

- Bill R. Gargano Sr., who arrived in Endicott from New York City in the mid-1940's as a twenty-something bursting with energy and ideas; Gargano would quickly assert himself as a contractor extraordinaire and a generous supporter of countless community endeavors.

- Douglas Whiting Burt, whose family's Burt Department Store emerged as an anchor of the Washington Avenue shopping district.

- Maurice F. Battisti, a restaurateur, builder, developer and selfless civic titan.

- John R. Brunner of Endicott Lumber & Box and then Endwell Homes Inc., who oversaw the construction of many houses throughout the village.

- James Kline, one of The Avenue's earliest and most prominent retail presences, whose Kline's Men's and Boy's store supplied local Boy Scouts with their official uniforms and equipment.

- Donald L. McManus, a printer who became Town of Union supervisor and later Broome County executive.

- Joseph A. Caldwell, mayor of Endicott from 1967 until 1977 and active in a host of civic, charitable and political organizations.

Names like Mersereau, Warner (a family that was prominent on the banking and insurance front), Burt and Kline are just a few of those synonymous with the growth of Endicott.

Within the sphere in which he operated, Coach Angeline's influence on life in Endicott was just as enormous and enduring as that of those other molders of the village. His impact was felt in all or parts of the last five decades of the 20th Century. Fittingly, the fieldhouse at Ty Cobb Stadium is now named after him. Under Coach Angeline's leadership, championship teams would roll forth from the high school just like great shoes and great adding machines came off the production lines at E-J and IBM. By the time U-E walloped Vestal, 42-8, on the frigid evening of November 7th, 1992, at Ty Cobb Stadium, drawing the curtain on an illustrious career, Angeline had earned resounding accolades from an adoring populace. Beyond that, he had touched thousands of lives in a positive way.

The 1960 ESS game was not one for the highlight reels. Instead it would go into the books as one of Angeline's most ignominious defeats. U-E lost, 40-7. Those of us who made the trip to Elmira groaned in agony as ESS' Jerry Reagan scored three touchdowns, helping the Green Hornets surge into a 27-0 lead at the half. We muttered in disbelief as our QB, Dave Sammon, threw one interception after another.

Amid the pallor of pending disaster, I detected at least one glimmer of light: several of U-E's underclassmen, most notably Bill Pickering, were showing signs of brilliance. Pickering accounted for U-E's only points on an eleven-yard run for a touchdown and a blast through the defensive line for the extra point. He also threw a fourth-down pass to Bobby Colburn from his fullback slot that produced a burst of clapping from the U-E cheering section. The drive that Pickering had kept alive stalled, though, when Sammon—definitely off his game—was tossed for a twelve-yard loss.

Always the optimist, I found reason for inspiration in the fact that Jerry Niles and John Dellos, both sophomores like myself, saw spot action behind Sammon at quarterback.

U-E was going down to its third loss in five starts. But maybe, just maybe, the Tigers would spring to life the following Saturday in Utica against Utica Proctor.

It would be a long week, waiting to find out.

Coach Angeline's son Chris (a future Tigers' quarterback), emulates his dad by holding a clipboard while sizing up Mark Seliga, left, and Mario Amorese, from U-E HS's '62 team.

ON THE ROAD AGAIN

Suddenly, the prospect of obtaining my learner's permit to drive a car, now less than a year away, loomed large. Throughout the early years of adolescence, graduating from pedal-powered to motorized transportation was not a prospect I had spent much time thinking about; I had become accustomed to galloping across great lengths of terrain on my bicycle. I could get anywhere in West Corners—Duffy's store, the playgrounds at the West Corners Elementary School, my friends' houses—in minutes. West Endicott wasn't much more of a strain. Leaping onto the seat of my bicycle like A.J. Foyt scrambling into position for the start of the Indianapolis 500, I was off and running. By the time I reached the bottom of the hill on Martin Street I had built up a full head of steam; the momentum I'd gathered carried me along Day Hollow Road to the old bridge over the Nanticoke Creek and onto the Union Maine Highway. Pumping hard, I would hit the West Endicott line with no loss of speed. That left only a flat stretch of Nanticoke Avenue between me and Jennings Street. Hooking a right onto Jennings Street, I would speed past Ideal Lanes on my right and my uncle's mill on my left and come to a screeching halt in my grandparents' driveway. By slamming on the brakes, I was able to cover the last several feet with a mean skid. The sound of rubber burning against pavement announced my arrival.

My bicycle took me to downtown Union, to the Boy's Club and the George F. Johnson Memorial Library and to Washington Avenue.

No one I knew was more attached to a bicycle than me. I was wed to it. I traveled far and wide, pausing just long enough to provide my mother with a loose approximation of where I was headed before setting out. Regardless of the destination, when I got there, I parked the bike by tilting it slightly so that one of the handlebars lay against the side of a secure resting place: my Grampa Lee's house; the window of a storefront on The Avenue; the chain-link fence surrounding the merry-go-round at West Endicott Park; a tree. I rarely used a bike rack. Sometimes I just threw the bike down, as if to say, "Stay there and behave."

I had removed the kickstand the moment the bike came home from Beaches, in Union. Kickstands were an impediment; they slowed you down. I never locked the bike. We didn't lock our house at night; there was no need to keep a bicycle under lock and key, either.

I'd ridden a bicycle for years and so had my friends. Any boy who didn't own one was a second-class citizen. I would no more have been without a bicycle than I would have sidled up to the dinner table without a knife, fork and spoon. Every kid I knew had a bicycle. Most of us souped up our bicycles by adding long plastic streamers to the leather grips; the streamers would snap, crackle and pop—like the cereal. The streamers—and baseball cards, attached to the spokes of the bicycle with clothespins—created an awful racket as we rumbled through the neighborhood. When we rode in packs, we resembled Jason and his pals from the movie E.T. except that we couldn't fly like they did at the end of the film.

Saturdays were my day to roam, and I took full advantage. Often I'd leave the house soon after getting out of bed, and be gone until after dark (this was especially true if there were chores to do!). My parents didn't worry because they knew I was probably at West Corners Elementary School. That was where my friends and I spent most of our leisure-time hours—engaged in a pick-up game of baseball, football or basketball. We carted our equipment, such as it was, around with us. Sticking a basketball or football under our left arm—which meant we had to guide our bicycles with our one free hand—was the recommended way of getting our gear to where we were going. We traveled light, bringing only what we needed. We fished baseballs out of the woods and the creek until they were too waterlogged or tattered to do us any good. We shared a catcher's mask. Sometimes we shared gloves and bats. When baseball season ended, we played full-bore tackle football without helmets or pads. I can still feel the thrill of snaring a pass from Mike Stone over the middle—or airing one out when I played quarterback and seeing the ball lead Tom Giordano so perfectly that he didn't have to break stride as he caught it and galloped toward the end zone. The end zone was always an imaginary line: a line extended out from a tree or some other rooted marker.

The robins and my friends and I arrived at the school about the same time every spring, the birds probing the soft, wet ground for earthworms, the rest of us scattering our Adirondack and Spalding bats in a pile next to the backstop in anticipation of the game that was about to take place (at fifteen, I loved wearing sweatshirts that were cut off at the shoulders, to show off my developing biceps). Of the two baseball diamonds available to us, we liked the one away from the creek best. The one nearest the creek was an annoyance; whenever a ball was fouled back, it meant scaling the fence to the rear and scrambling through prickly bushes on the embankment to retrieve it, or picking it out of the gurgling waters of the Nanticoke. Our field of choice, across the way, featured an open area behind the backstop, making foul balls more easily retrievable. It was also fenced in the outfield, so that there was no confusion about whether someone had hit a legitimate home run. Whenever a ball cleared the fence and bounced around in the stand of trees behind it, the player could "touch them all," as John Fogarty would put it so evocatively in his baseball song "Centerfield." Having a fence to aim at was the far more preferable arrangement; in baseball, as in life, one wants measurable distances by which to gauge ability.

The basketball court at the school was one of only two surfaced full-length outdoor courts in all of West Corners. The other was a concrete court that Dr. Giordano had created in the woods deep behind his home for his sons, Vince and Tom, and their comrades to enjoy.

I had already honed my talents to a sharp edge on our driveway on Hazel Avenue, shooting at the iron hoop attached to a ply-wood backboard that my dad had mounted over the garage door. There, often all by myself, I had spent hours in the sun, rain, sleet and wind, trying to emulate the particular skill my favorite NBA players were noted for. One day, pretending I was Bob Cousy, the floor general of the Boston Celtics, I'd practice dribbling away the final seconds of a game while pretend defenders scrambled in desperation to catch me, their fingers stabbing at thin air just like those who tried to get the ball away from "the Houdini of the Hardwood." At such moments, I could almost hear their coaches and their fans berating these hapless souls for their futility.

Another day, picturing myself as Bob Pettit, the star of the St. Louis Hawks, I would attempt running right-handed hook shots. Or, copying Oscar Robertson of the Cincinnati Royals, I would dribble toward the hoop with my back to the basket to keep the ball away from the man guarding me, then feint right and, turn-ing left and going airborne at the same time, let loose an arching jump shot. In doing so, I would cock my right wrist just like "The

Big O" and release the ball with a soft reverse spin. Sometimes I'd pretend I was Wilt Chamberlain of the Philadelphia Warriors, letting the ball roll off the tips of my fingers in an attempt to duplicate his celebrated scoop shot, or banking the ball off the backboard as I fell away from the basket as I'd seen "Wilt the Stilt" do it on TV. Or I'd be Jerry West of the Los Angeles Lakers, running and gunning.

At home, the extent to which I was able to perfect these moves was dictated by the limited space I had to work with: our driveway was only about ten feet wide. There was little room in which to operate. The Giordanos' court seemed immense by comparison; there, I could thread a pinpoint pass to a teammate, shoot from deep on the side or lead a fast break in the other direction. In this more favorable setting I was able to demonstrate all of the techniques I'd learned on Hazel Avenue. Between the two places, I improved. Soon I was the second-best best player in the neighborhood after Tommy Giordano. I was ready to take my show to a bigger stage: the Boy's Club in Endicott, where I proceeded to light up the nets under the watchful eye of "Slim" Sylvester; and then to Jennie F. Snapp where I won a spot on the freshman squad.

U-E's football team would undertake some serious roving too, during the Angeline years. Trips took the Tigers well beyond the Triple Cities and even the Southern Tier. This adventurousness stemmed in part from reconfigurations of the conference that left big schools like U-E and Vestal looking to fill open slots on their schedules. A lot of the area's smaller schools were reluctant to tangle with the Tigers and the Bears. U-E and Vestal's tendency to roam arose too, though, from an eagerness to show the rest of the state how tough and talented the Tier's top teams were. The upcoming game at Utica Proctor was one of those encounters that took the Tigers away from the den to foreign soil.

There would be so many such far-flung forays in the future that Willie Nelson's "On The Road Again" would have been an appropriate choice as the Tigers' theme song. Some of these were regular-season encounters. Some occurred in the post season. They literally took Angeline's teams from one end of the state to the other. Although winning away from home is always a difficult proposition in any league, U-E seemed to relish the challenge. Tiger teams certainly savored the opportunity to make a statement on the road. Nothing got Angeline's teams charged up more than sticking it to the hosts on the other guys' turf. Nothing was sweeter than the specter of an unfriendly crowd being struck mute by the shellacking its darlings were being subjected to at the hands of the Orange and Black.

At no time was U-E's road-warrior prowess put to a sterner test than during Angeline's swan-song campaign, in 1992. That year, the Tigers logged more than one thousand miles, round trip, over the course of four consecutive weekends with forays to Shenendehowa (in the Clifton Park/Schenectady area), Middletown, Pine Bush (both in Orange County, downstate) and finally to Elmira Southside. That U-E was willing to venture away from the familiar confines of Ty Cobb Stadium week after week that fall underscored the Athletic Department's confidence in the school's high-powered football program. That the Tigers won all four of those outings proved they were as punishing a force to reckon with in opponents' own backyard as they were on the banks of the Susquehanna.

Heading east out of Binghamton with a carload of my buddies for the game at Utica Proctor on the last Saturday in October of 1960, I was overcome by the thrill of feeling footloose. This was the farthest from home I'd gone without my parents at the wheel. Ahead of us on Route 12, the school buses carrying the coaches and players and cheerleaders appeared to pulsate with nervous energy as we made our way through New Berlin and Norwich. It was a scene that would be repeated many times over in the years to follow as Tiger teams climbed aboard buses on Fridays and Saturdays for games against non-league foes.

Some of the meetings that materialized as a result of this practice would go into the record books as classics. U-E's '82 game at Rome Free Academy was one of these: a collision of the state's No. 1 and No. 2-ranked teams with a crowd of 13,000 shouting itself hoarse in an attempt to influence the outcome. Though U-E was armed with such marquee players as Alex Rita, Joe Mott and swift-footed Bobby Norris that year, the Tigers lost, 8-7. The next year, 1983, U-E paid a visit to what Angeline, in his autobiography, referred to as the "Kingston Zoo": Dietz Stadium. Not only was there an actual zoo on the premises, a zoo-like atmosphere prevailed. When Angeline remarked to a Kingston supporter that one of the hosts' players "could pass for being in his mid-twenties," he was informed, "oh, he's a P.G. (a post-graduate student)…just taking a few courses." Kingston apparently didn't "know" that "P.G.'s" had been banned in New York state since the early 1950's!

During Angeline's tenure, there were memorable battles with Buffalo's Bishop Timon Catholic, a trip north in '84 to help Liverpool christen its new stadium (U-E lost, 20-0), and a return in '90 to Kingston's Dietz Stadium to face Warwick in a Regional title clash. U-E turned that game into what Angeline called "a big-league trip" by heading south early. The Tigers won the collision, 28-7.

In '89, U-E capped one of the sweetest seasons in school history—a perfect 11-0 campaign—with back-to-back playoff wins on successive weekends over Corning East and Monroe-Woodbury at Schoellkopf Field on the campus of Cornell University, high above Cayuga Lake. No Tiger team ever performed more brilliantly on the road than the '89 squad, especially the last two weeks. Against Corning East's Trojans on the Astroturf in Cornell's spacious crescent stadium in the Section 4 Bowl 1 title game, U-E's Markus Wilson, Jarvis Shields and Paul Norris reeled off 61, 77 and 28-yard touchdowns, respectively. U-E won, 21-19. The following weekend, facing Monroe-Woodbury, from Section IX in Orange County, in the Class A Regional title game, U-E QB Chris Waters scored four touchdowns. U-E romped, 54-13.

The '89 season had been a season rivaled by only one other: '79. Week after week in '89 the Tigers vanquished foes as if they were stepping on ants: Kingston, 20-0; Bishop Timon Catholic, 60-7; Elmira Free Academy, 32-14; Binghamton North, 35-26; Johnson City, 49-6; Elmira Southside, 54-0; Ithaca, 40-13; and finally Vestal, 23-6, to complete the regular season.

In 1960, as members of a new sophomore class at U-E struggled to fit in, Angeline and his staff were already working hard to develop a football program that would rekindle Endicotters' interest. Through the first five games of the season, there had been signs of progress.

For a while that day in Utica, it looked like U-E would snap its two-game losing skid and that the ride back to Endicott would be a raucously festive one. Utica Proctor, however, spoiled the scenario by scoring three times in the fourth quarter to finish off a 26-0 triumph.

I took solace in John Dellos' effort. Our classmate, "The Quiet Man," who walked the halls of school as if tiptoeing his way through a hospital zone, who in his unassuming and unpretentious and almost-bashful way projected none of the jock presence of a Bobby Atkinson or Ken Pacioni or Joe Conrad or Dick Streno, had gained seventy-four yards against Utica Proctor. Dellos was one of the few bright spots that afternoon, and it gave the Class of '63 some comfort to see one of our own demonstrate such skill. Except for John Dellos and Bill Pickering (the latter got off several booming punts), there was little for U-E to crow about.

Returning home, Endicott never looked better to me. The high school—the one I'd found so forbidding at first—now appeared ready to welcome me into its strong and comforting arms. The Avenue beckoned; I knew, come Monday, I'd be making a stop at the lunch counter at Woolworth's for a cheeseburger or a visit to Woody's for a Fats Domino "45" or to the Elk's Bake Shop for a creamy cinnamon bun.

I was despondent nevertheless. The Tigers now stood 2-and-4. The bloom was off the rose; autumn's chill felt colder than it should have. And now there were only two games left in the '60 season.

"Is it possible," I wondered, "that there will be no escaping the doldrums we'd experienced in '59"—after Nick DiNunzio had replaced "Ty" Cobb at the helm? That exhiliration would give way, again and again, to dejection as the Tigers fumbled and sputtered their way to defeat?

Is it conceivable, I wondered, that Coach Angeline will fail in his attempt to orchestrate a rejuvenation?

The EFA game, seven days away, would provide the answer.

En-Joie Pool, where I learned to swim. It held one million gallons of water but was demolished in the 1960's, never to be replaced.

Mentors and "Devils"

I did not think for a minute in 1960, as my mother turned the page of our Magic City Ice Co. wall calendar from October to November, that Endicott would follow the path of other pre-eminent places and slide into The Great Abyss. I was still largely ignorant in the matter of the rise and fall of civilizations. The end of the village's heyday was near. Its run as a socioeconomic juggernaut would, when all was said and done, have lasted for less than three quarters of a century: a kernel of sand in the hourglass of time. I was unaware of this, although the clues lay all around me.

Earlier that year, Endicott-Johnson had announced that it was expanding its shoe-manufacturing operation to Mississippi in order to produce a line of women's shoes not being made in its twenty-five plants in the Triple Cities and northern Pennsylvania. The handwriting was on the wall; all too soon, E-J would pull up stakes completely. E-J's ultimate departure would be a crippling blow to the village. Like a chicken that has had its head chopped off, Endicott would be lost without Endicott-Johnson. E-J's exit would signal the beginning of the end for Endicott as an industrial powerhouse.

Also in 1960, a heated dispute erupted when a plan was put forth in the village to eliminate diagonal parking on Washington Avenue. The scheme called for parallel parking instead, which meant that The Avenue would lose about two-thirds of its parking spaces. Most of The Avenue's merchants were incensed. Shopkeepers like Lee Herr of Lee's Dress Shop and John Chipper of Endicott Shoe expressed bitter opposition. Many of the people doing business on The Avenue—bankers, clothiers, jewelers, druggists—viewed the potential elimination of diagonal parking with alarm. They understood—correctly—that any change that made it harder for shoppers to get to their doorstep was bad policy.

In 1960, winds of change, situated at the very edge of the village, were gathering strength. Soon they would blow through with a sinister design, leaving in their wake a veritable wasteland. E-J's factories would disappear. Historic properties associated with the E-J years would vanish. Thousands of jobs would go out the window. Washington Avenue—the most conspicuous symbol of the village's prosperity—would plunge into decline. E-J and Washington Avenue had risen as one; they would fade as one as well. As the fixture businesses vacated their spots, one by one—Woolworth's, Levinson's, Newberry's, Dwyer's Shoes, Georgia-Hanks, Hilkins Jewelers, Woody's, McLean's, Burt's, the Dave Lewis Shoe Market, Kline's, the National Army & Navy, Endicott Textile, the Strand and the Lyric theaters, Sacks Sales, the Tri-Phi Shops, Henry's Tobacco, the Singer Sewing Center, Zappia's and on and on—residents of the village would shake their heads in lament. There was nothing they could do; they were like a field of hay being flattened by a force beyond their control.

During my three years at Union-Endicott High School, concluding with the graduation of my class on the floor of Ty Cobb

Stadium on a warm day in June of '63, I learned a great deal about the pendulum-like nature of life. I received this instruction in the classroom, and outside of it. I would learn that even the mightiest of nations and the strongest of men fall by the wayside in due course.

Gradually, what I was being taught at West Endicott Baptist Church and in school sank in: man, and earth, would ultimately wither and die. Only God would remain. Man is mortal; God is eternal.

My run-in with Mr. Nicosia had put me in my place. Until that moment no adult except my father and my Grandma Blossom had laid a hand on me in anger. Once, my dad, a mild-mannered man who seldom lost his temper, abruptly and savagely pulled our car to the side of the road. Then he dove into the back seat to pummel my brothers and me, for acting up. Another time, my grandmother took a "switch" from the woods behind her house to my bare legs as I stood at the front door. It was her way of reprimanding me for my incessant wailing that my parents had abandoned us. They had simply traveled to Cleveland for a few days to visit my Aunt Bessie and her husband Frank.

My encounter with Russ Nicosia had taught me humility. I had developed a big head in West Corners. I had made the frosh basketball team at Jennie F. Snapp. I had won the affection of Laurene Perfetti. I considered myself invincible. I was overdue for a whip lashing, and Russ Nicosia was more than willing to administer it. Nicosia was a graduate of the State University of New York at Brockport (SUNY Brockport): a school known for its athletics. He was an impetuous, physical man. Long after our run-in, whenever I came across the photograph in my Class of '63 Thesaurus of Coach Angeline and his staff, my eyes would linger on the image of Mr. Nicosia and my cheeks would flush. Throughout the years to follow, whenever successes accrued and my cockiness reached insufferable levels, I knew instinctively that a Russ Nicosia would be waiting in the wings to knock me down a peg or two. The roughing up I'd received from him would not be my last. It would, however, teach me that it is not wise to get "too big for your britches," as my Grandma Blossom would say.

The administrators, coaches and teachers with whom I came into contact at U-E reinforced my notion that Endicott boasted more than its share of achievers and role models. From the moment I entered the matronly Mrs. Robbins' first-grade class at West Corners Elementary School in September of 1950 and began to write cursive until I set off for Fredonia State College, far upstate, in the fall of '63, educators—like my family and friends—were as much the face of Endicott to me as the statue of George F. Johnson, the E-J Workers Arch, the En-Joie pool and the merry-go-round at West Endicott Park.

Not all of the academic persons I met bought into the hysteria that enveloped the high school soon after Coach Angeline reported for work and started to rebuild a football program that was in shambles. For some of my teachers, the idea of pep rallies, bonfires and shouting encouragement to the Tigers on Saturday nights was either infantile or just plain inconsequential to the crucial business of education. Either way, in their view appearances at Ty Cobb Stadium were a waste of their precious time. They would no sooner have attended a U-E football game than they would have shown up at a sock hop at the JC Rec or walked into Woody's on The Avenue to buy a copy of Johnny Rivers' new hit song "Secret Agent Man" or "Rock Around the Clock," by Bill Haley's Comets.

By the time I returned to school in September of 1962 for the start of my senior year, several older acquaintances had briefed me in thorough fashion on one of these "eggheads:" Dennis Bottino, whose College Preparatory (CP) English class I was about to enter. By then, having flunked tryouts for both the varsity basketball and varsity baseball teams, I had turned my insatiable appetite for sports to the game of golf. My preoccupation with it was total; as the clock wound towards mid-afternoon and the clang of the last bell, my only thought was about getting out of the building quickly and hooking up with my cousin, Clarence Fowler, who lived almost directly across the street from En-Joie Golf Club, for a quick nine holes. Or, better yet, eighteen holes. No teacher could interest me in anything but adhering to this regimen. Or so I thought.

Clarence Fowler was my first mentor in the game. Others— Nick Legnini, Al Morley, Tex Dudek and John Becker at IBM Country Club and Bob Klink and Tommy Kuhn at Binghamton Country Club (for all of whom I later worked)—would follow. All were card-carrying members of the Professional Golfers Association (PGA) except for Dudek. All were true hustlers, in the spirit of "Slammin" Sammy Snead or "Super Mex" Lee Trevino, when it came to taking money from novices like me. I lost small change putting for pennies, nickels and dimes with Tommy Kuhn (the assistant pro at BCC) and John Marsh (who ran the caddie shack there) on the putting green at Binghamton Country Club, where our impromptu "matches" after we'd finished for the day often didn't end until we were enshrouded in darkness. Morley, Dudek and Becker emptied even bigger amounts from my pockets on IBM CC's championship course. At the feet of these ruthless "tutors" I improved until I was able to hold onto some of my money. Nothing turns a hacker into a lower-handicap player faster than the prospect of seeing his meager wages flutter away like wisps of smoke as the loser in a five-dollar Nassau.

My cousin Clarence, a natural at everything he did, enjoyed only one thing more than hitting the ball long and straight and matching or beating par at En-Joie, and that was whirling around the course in record time. I was always rushing to catch up. It was not unusual for the two of us, playing unaccompanied, to complete a round in two hours (I like to think it would have warmed George F. Johnson's heart to see his flat, easy-to-use track capitalized on in this fashion, exactly as he'd intended).

Clarence, a big-boned man and an unabashed striker of the ball, stepped up and hit each shot without a moment's pause, as if by way of saying, "He who hesitates is lost." This was true of tee shots, medium and short-iron shots, sand shops, chip shots and putts. They were all the same to him. His approach seemed to be, "the shortest distance between two points is a straight line; I'm going straight for the jugular."

When not on the attack, he was charging down the fairway, his handcart dragging along behind—but always several steps ahead of me. He would stop only to impart some tidbit of advice, as for instance when he uttered the admonition "never up, never in," whenever I left a putt short of the hole. Limp putts were a cardinal sin to Clarence. Until he died prematurely, Clarence was one of En-Joie Golf Club's lowest-scoring players. If he didn't par a hole, it was usually because he had birdied it.

Like En-Joie's other "paid" season-pass members, Clarence relished the privilege of having access to the course whenever he wanted, and he resented having to relinquish his home club for a week every year to the B.C. Open—a stop on the PGA Tour. He was far less interested in seeing Ben Crenshaw, Tom Watson, Joey Sindelar, Raymond Floyd or even Arnold Palmer in action than he was in finding out whether he could "run the table" and shoot 68. Hitting the ball better than the next guy, growing prize vegetables and riding his bicycle all over Union and West Endicott left Clarence little time, and little inclination, for following the fluctuating fortunes of the world's best players.

Clarence was a modern-day Renaissance Man, proficient in every activity and project he undertook. The trappings of his own life were enough for him. I wanted to be just like him.

— ❖ —

It was easy for me to understand why Clarence appreciated what George F. Johnson had done for the community. En-Joie—the public course Johnson created for E-J workers and that he allowed anyone to play for a quarter—had given Clarence countless hours of pleasure. Like other dues-paying members, Clarence considered En-Joie to be his. He knew every blade of grass and grain of sand on the course. Stepping up to a tee, he never had to think twice about which club to use; the yardages and various pin placements were imbedded in his brain. Walking the course, he'd holler or wave or nod to someone one fairway over. It was the same in the clubhouse afterwards. Clarence loped up the steps into the grill room with an effortless motion and was as comfortable talking golf over drinks at one of the wooden tables there as he was relaxing in the parlor of his E-J house on Paden Street, one block away.

At one time Clarence worked in maintenance/housekeeping at two of the other valued properties George F. Johnson had provided the village: the Hotel Frederick on The Avenue and Ideal Hospital, high on the hill above the Susquehanna River. Clarence's association with these two institutions—each vitally connected to life in Endicott by way of their role as places for social gatherings (in the case of the Frederick) and for births, deaths and medical treatment (in the case of Ideal Hospital)—deepened his respect for George F. Johnson's enormous contributions to the village. As a busboy, I worked with Clarence for a time at the Hotel Frederick, where when he wasn't changing light bulbs or swabbing floors he was flirting with the waitresses. After we'd both left the Frederick, I often sought him out at Ideal Hospital, where, because the place was so big, I'd have to ride the elevator up and down to find him.

The Hotel Frederick, of course, fell to the wrecking ball; it was another of Endicott's symbols from the George F. Johnson era that would be rudely snatched from us. Ideal Hospital, meanwhile, was ultimately closed down as a medical facility and turned into a home for the elderly. In their heyday both had been spectacular and seemingly indispensable buildings. Not so spectacular or indispensable, apparently, to be considered untouchable. The loss of the Hotel Frederick and Ideal Hospital was hard for Endicotters to accept; or to understand.

It would have crushed my cousin Clarence to see En-Joie Golf Club meet a similar fate. Yet it almost happened. Developers almost latched onto the golf course when E-J was selling off its surplus properties. Disaster was averted in the nick of time; although presented with a lucrative offer by the would-be new owners, E-J sold the acreage instead to the village of Endicott at a bargain price, assuring that the 6,150-yard links would continue to be used in the manner George F. Johnson had envisioned for it for years to come.

Johnson died too soon to witness the start-up of the B.C. Open as a "satellite" tournament in the early 1970's. He died too soon to see Richie Karl, a hometown boy, who'd grown up on Swartwood Avenue, abutting the course, win the 1974 B.C. Open in a sudden-death playoff, with the roar of thousands of exultant fans from throughout Broome County ringing in his ears as he closed out Australian Bruce Crampton. Although the clubhouse in which Clarence and I shared so many carefree moments burned to the ground earlier that year, the '74 tournament was held as scheduled. Better yet, En-Joie Golf Club lived…and so escaped the fate that befell so many other remnants of the E-J/George F. Johnson years.

Throughout my high school years, golf distracted me from my studies; my grades seemed to drop proportionate to every stroke I took off my score at En-Joie. No teacher could divert my attention from the sport I now embraced with an all-consuming fervor. Not the balding, bow tie-wearing Mr. (Charles) Turver, who taught Biology. Not the black rimmed-spectacled, wavy-haired

Mr. (Carl) Zonio, who taught French. Not the gregarious and opinionated Mr. (Vincent) Giarusso, who taught World History. Not the animated, burly and engaging Mr. (Frank) Sorochinsky, who taught Chemistry. Not even the diffident Mr. (Charles) Kasky, from whom I took Driver's Ed. Except for Intramural Basketball, no extracurricular activities caught my fancy as I made my way from class to class, teacher to teacher, year to year. I was hurt that I was no longer part of the athletic elite, and it showed.

Classmates would avail themselves of the many opportunities available to us for self-discovery. Sexy Bernadette Tovornik would become president of the Leaders Club. The shy but erudite Fred Cosin would become editor-in-chief of the school newspaper, the *Tornado*. My friend Bill Thayer would attach himself to many organizations, including the Model UN and the Debate Club. Anne Marie Wahila, Fred Cosin, Janet Beach, Mike Nalevanko, Jerry Albrecht, Jerry Niles, Bob Smith, Tom Giordano, Norma Southworth and Dave Sipko would all emerge as pillars of the National Honor Society. Josie Shady would join the French Club. I drifted along, blind to much of what was happening around me as I crossed paths in the hallways with U-E's administrators...Superintendent of Schools Robert D. Agone, Principal Martin Bortnick Jr., Vice Principal Michael E. Gance, and the school's faculty and staff...Mr. (Joe) Kazlauskas, Mr. (Robert) Barno, Mr. (Edward) Goodnow, Mr. (Frank) Huggins, Mr. (Bruce) Ellis, Miss (Adona) Sick. I sensed that I was becoming a source of exasperation for my guidance counselors, Mr. (Julius) George and Ms. (Roberta) Scott, because of my reluctance to get involved, even as I conferred with them about the prospect of continuing my education beyond high school.

Walking The Avenue, hanging out with my friends, following the exploits of U-E's sports teams and playing golf were all I cared about my first two years in high school.

Then I began my senior year and met Mr. Bottino.

Despite what I'd heard about Mr. Bottino's skills as a teacher and a motivator, I was certain his class, my last of the afternoon, would be just another "session" I'd have to tolerate until I could make the dash from the third floor of the building down the stairs and out the door to En-Joie. When I saw that the desk I'd been assigned was on the outside wall, with a great view of East Main Street looking toward the monument of George F. Johnson, I rejoiced; at least I could daydream about winning the Broome County Amateur or the Utica Open while the monotony ensued.

It took a rendezvous with a non-conformist of Mr. Bottino's ilk to change all that. Mr. Bottino was not a particularly attractive man; his most conspicuous characteristics—short, hairy arms, a dark complexion and a pug face—brought to mind the combative governor of Alabama: George C. Wallace. Dennis Bottino's nonchalant disregard for convention was inspiring, however; he challenged all of the procedural dictums bossy administrators fired his way, from the stipulation that he had to attend assemblies to the order that he had to wear a tie, dismissing each and every one as "silly."

The poets—Byron, Keats and Shelley, Wordsworth, John Donne, the Brownings, Walt Whitman, Robert Frost—and their work, were another matter. They were to be taken seriously. The exuberance with which Mr. Bottino discussed their thoughts and writings energized the room. The way he read passages from their poems, or whole poems—with joie de vivre—kindled in his students a desire to hear more. His call for a penetrating examination of the style and substance of the poet's contemplations rallied young minds to a bold new undertaking. His dissertations on the lives of the poets, his probing analysis of their "take" on life and their proclaimed "truths," fired the imagination of his students and whetted their appetite for self-expression. Mr. Bottino forced his students out of their shell. He challenged them to think critically. He taught them to accept no premise without examining it from every angle for the slightest hint of falsity or weakness.

Mr. Bottino's affinity for the dissidents manifested itself in references to Henry David Thoreau's refusal to pay taxes and Mahatma Gandhi's espousal of the merits of civil disobedience. In his class the great poets, thinkers and writers provided the sounding board for penetrating discussions of beauty, good, justice and truth. Each period spent with Mr. Bottino took his students into territory they had never explored. It was serious work leavened with occasional episodes of comedic relief. Periodically Mr. Sorochinsky would wander by, pause at the door of Mr. Bottino's room, and begin a lively repartee with Mr. Bottino. I did not know how they'd become friends. They seemed like total opposites. Mr. Bottino was immersed in the business of verse and the exploration of hidden literary caves; Mr. Sorochinsky was wrapped up in the study of chemical compositions. Mr. Bottino held no readily apparent interest in athletics; Mr. Sorochinsky was an assistant football coach and head wrestling coach. Their teaching styles were different too. Mr. Bottino stood at the front of the room: a short man, beseeching and cajoling and lecturing. Mr. Sorochinsky restlessly wandered the rows of his class in his imitable rocking walk: a big man looking very much like a bear on the prowl (the better to impose a presence and to get a bird's-eye view of a student's paperwork). Despite these differences, in their animated exchanges it was apparent that they had a lot in common—not the least of which was an affinity for dialogue of the sort that would keep Mr. Bottino's students in stitches.

In the days leading up to the Tigers' seventh game of the '60 season, Mr. Bottino's CP English class—still two years away—was the furthest thing from my mind. It's fair to assume also that the Tigers' exploits to that point—two wins and four defeats, including three defeats in a row—were, likewise, of small concern to Mr. Bottino. Most everyone else knew that with only two starts left, the Tigers needed a magnificent showing against Elmira Free Academy's Blue Devils to set the stage for a victory over Binghamton Central in the '60 season finale to finish 4-4 in Coach Angeline's first season at the switch. A tie or a loss would represent a bad omen indeed.

Saturday, November 5th, 1960, dawned cold, a hint that winter in Endicott was near at hand. I was not eager to climb out of bed. Instead, I snuggled deeper into the blanket, catching what warmth I could as my mother and father's feet pattered up and down the hallway between their bedroom and the kitchen. The game was hours away. I could afford the luxury of sleeping in.

U-E fans did not know what to expect as the kickoff approached. The only thing that seemed certain was that the collision was going to be played out in Ice Bowl-like conditions; the temperature was dropping by the hour. What this would mean for the Tigers' suddenly impotent offense, which had produced only 14 points to opponents' 86 in U-E's three most recent outings, was anyone's guess.

In the years to follow, covering my alma mater's games, home and away, as a sportswriter for the *Press & Sun-Bulletin*, I experienced few days or nights more frigid than the one we were dealt for the EFA clash. Cold of the kind that settles across the Southern Tier come fall and winter is something players, coaches, fans and the press get used to. Especially in late October and early November, the chill can settle deep into your bones by the time the game has ended. Such was the cold that greeted us that day.

The Tigers, though, wasted no time warming up to their task. The turnaround from their most recent performances was astounding. Fired up by the early slashing runs of Bobby Colburn, George Wallace and Dick Pugh, they seized command with a vengeance. By the end of the game—a resounding 46-13 victory—they had amassed 431 yards' total offense. The defense was just as sharp, accounting for three fumble recoveries and three interceptions.

It seemed like everyone got into the act, which was the best part of all for the Class of '63: with regular QB Dave Sammon playing one of his finest games ever in the Orange and Black, sophomore John Dellos saw extended action and came through brilliantly for the second straight week. My fellow sophomores Bobby Atkinson and Jim Michael starred as well.

John Dellos and Dick Pugh collaborated on a 17-yard touchdown pass in the second quarter. Dellos ran in a TD himself from six yards out in the fourth quarter. Bobby Atkinson added a two-yard run for a TD and Bill Pickering boomed the extra point through the uprights to close out U-E's scoring.

The EFA game may well have been the outing that put the Tigers on the right track for the many memorable seasons that would follow under Fran Angeline. It certainly put them in good shape to finish the '60 campaign with a win over Binghamton Central and return respectability to U-E's beleaguered program.

On The Avenue on Monday, my friends and I felt warmth ooze back into our bodies as we talked excitedly about the Tigers' impressive showing.

Life was good again.

George F. Johnson's home on Park Street in Endicott, which was turned into the public library after his death. Sadly and despite fierce community consternation, it was torn down.

THE TIGER GROWLS AGAIN

As U-E center Rich Vivona, a gifted football player, and the rest of the Tigers resumed practice on Monday, it was still by no means certain that the infuriatingly inconsistent '60 team could cap the season with a victory over Binghamton Central. Nor was it yet obvious to those who'd lost confidence in the U-E football program during its hibernation that Angeline was the one to reawaken the savage in our gridders. There was more reason than usual for optimism, however: we had shellacked EFA in our last outing; the hapless Bulldogs, meanwhile, were winless for the year, at 0-and-7.

As a kid I'd heard stories about the vaunted U-E teams of yesteryear: the 1920's; 1930's; and 1940's. Based on these accounts from my dad and others, I had grown up with images of an "Orange tornado" swirling onto the turf like the armies of William the Conqueror or Attila the Hun and mowing down opponents as if they were so many toy soldiers. As a boy, it was easy for me to visualize the action unfolding on the scarred turf of Ty Cobb Stadium on Saturday afternoons: our big, lumbering players, many of them "P.G.'s," or post graduates (as the stories went), arrayed in a single wing or "I" or "T" formation on the field of battle...the snap of the ball...the sweep of massive, dull-witted, partially bearded linemen right or left to lead the charge...the whoosh of tough backs through the tackle hole or around the end and on down the sidelines toward the end zone...the referee thrusting two arms overhead...thunderous applause erupting.

Still vivid in my mind was the sight of Tigers players hoisting Harold V. "Ty" Cobb onto their shoulders in November of 1958 after he'd coached his last game. He'd arrived in Endicott from Michigan around the time of World War I. He'd been U-E's coach for thirty-nine seasons, amassing 202 wins! He was an institution. Nick DiNunzio, who replaced "Ty" Cobb as coach in 1959, had played for him. So had Fran Angeline. Presidents, prime ministers and popes had come and gone; through it all there had been "Ty" Cobb. It was hard to imagine anyone else as coach.

Before long, U-E fans felt the same way about Angeline. By the time the people of Endicott gathered for a sold-out testimonal dinner for Angeline in February of '93, his own legacy was secure. Three months earlier, in November of '92, the forty-five members of his last team, their emotions whipped to a frenzy by an awareness that Angeline's coaching career was coming to an end, had snorted in unison in rumbling past Vestal, 42-8. Angeline, his gimpy knees so severely deteriorated from years of constant strain that he'd resorted to using a golf cart to ride out to the practice field, had logged his 216th win in his 311th and final game as a high school football coach.

It had been a week to remember. There had been telephone calls and visits from well-wishers, a boisterious pep rally at the Charles F. Johnson Elementary School, media hype, even a surprise article in the local newspaper the morning of the game: Angeline's daughter, the musically gifted and luminous Vaun Angeline, had collaborated from a distance (California) with Charlie Jaworski, the executive sports editor of the *Press and Sun-Bulletin*, to pen a personal tribute to her father for the newspaper. The headline read: "Football or not, dad's little girl loves the coach."

Vaun Angeline was unable to attend the Vestal game. She was present in February, however, when the sendoff for her father took place. So too were hundreds of others, defying a Nor'easter that had struck the Triple Cities that day: U-E Superintendent Richard "Dick" McLean, who served as master of ceremonies; former coaching rivals Dick Hoover of Vestal, Joe Moresco of Ithaca and Paul Munley of Johnson City; members of Angeline's staff; Bob Gallagher (a colleague and friend); family; neighbors; fans; boosters.

When it came time to deliver his parting remarks, Angeline sounded much like Gen. Douglas MacArthur returning to West Point one last time. He closed with words that had a military ring to them:

"What does one say to so many? While I am very appreciative of such generosity, please know that your fellowship and contact diminish everything else. These shall endure forever. As I reflect, I realize that I have been associated with this great game of ours, as both a player and a coach, for almost forty-five years. That's almost a lifetime! But it's now time for me to move on. I do not know what the future holds. I want you to know, however, that I'll miss all of you. And wherever I am, when the leaves begin to fall and there's a slight chill in the air, my finest thoughts will always be of the Orange and Black."

U-E defeated Binghamton Central, 14-6, on that second Saturday in November, 1960. By doing so, the Tigers had accomplished more in Angeline's first year than many had thought possible. Little did U-E fans know that the 1960 team's 4-4 finish was just the beginning of a forty-karat-gold chapter in U-E football annals, and in the village's history.

The field at Ty Cobb Stadium, softened and worn from a season's battering, had turned treacherous as U-E and Central prepared to clash. Despite the awful footing, Bobby Colburn cut the Bulldogs' line to shreds in his final game. It was a fitting conclusion to a spectacular senior season for Colburn. From the moment he grabbed a perfectly pitched lateral from Dave Sammon in the first quarter to score from the five yard line, Colburn drove the Bulldogs crazy. He rushed eleven times for sixty-eight yards. For the year, he averaged more than six yards per carry! It was the kind of stat that brought to mind the brilliant running of a much bigger and much stronger running back of the time: the Cleveland Browns' Jim Brown.

As we took our seats for the game, my pals nodded in agreement when I blurted out the prediction that U-E football teams would "dazzle" the experts in the years to come. These friends, long-time cronies from West Corners like Bobby Muir, shared my conviction that U-E would rise again. Bobby and I were sports junkies. In Bobby's case, even speech and hearing deformities that made it difficult for him to talk and carry on a conversation could not dull his enthusiasm for "the game." Growing up, we spent hours trading baseball cards, playing "pepper" in his front yard, or mine, and listening to Mel Allen and "Red" Barber call the Yankee games on the radio. With each change of season, we'd switch gears and keep on playing, driven by the dream that we would be big stars ourselves at U-E one day.

My instincts about a resurgence of "the Tiger" in U-E football teams proved to be correct. In the 1960's, as first Endicott-Johnson and then Washington Avenue began their slow but inevitable decline, U-E football, under Fran Angeline's direction, started its trek to the top of the mountain.

Many of the landmarks for which Endicott had become famous were, by 1960, gone or in the process of disappearing forever; among them, the "Endicott Restaurant" (actually four restaurants), where eleven thousand meals a day were served to E-J workers. Also the Fine Welt Factory, which employed more than twenty-six hundred workers and which turned out nearly twenty-three thousand pairs of men's and boy's dress shoes a day; and the Chrome Sole Leather Tannery, which boasted almost two acres of floor space and two hundred employees, and which accounted for eighteen hundred sides of leather a day. The towering smoke-stacks of the E-J "Power House," defining the Endicott skyline, would be ingloriously erased as well.

In 1960 came the sad news too that the Endicott Boy's Club on Broad Street would be closed; a new, bigger Boy's Club, eventually to be given the name the Louis N. Picciano Sr. Boy's Club of Endicott (after the man who took charge of a floundering hardware and plumbing business around 1929 and turned it into a winner), would be constructed in the "stable area" of En-Joie Park just east of Ty Cobb Stadium. The new Boy's Club, designed to accommodate boys and girls, was to be built on piers, to keep the structure safe from flooding that occurred whenever the Susquehanna River overflowed its banks.

The old Endicott Boy's Club had been my home away from home. I don't know how many times I bounded up the front steps and through the front door, there to discover, in its tall hallway and numerous rooms, activities to satisfy a youth's insatiable appetite for fun and games. I had honed my basketball skills in the gym annex that was added to the club in the 1950's. I had heard "Slim" Sylvester, who ran the facility with tender loving care, tell me more than once, after I'd "smoked" an opposing team for twenty or more points, that I was as "pure" a shooter as he'd seen. To learn in 1960 that the club would have to give way to a replacement building, albeit an improved one, was not what I wanted to hear. I was thunderstruck, and filled with regret.

The village I'd known as a youth was unraveling, like a ball of yarn. At the same time, Fran Angeline had come along, like Mighty Mouse, to save the U-E football program from a similar demise.

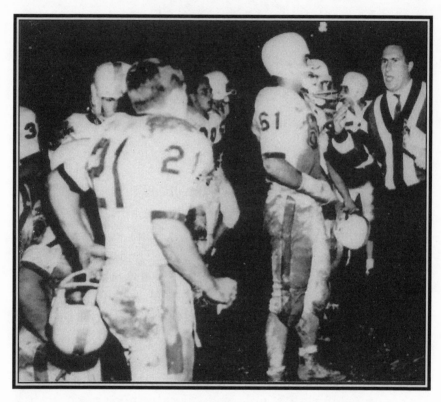

Coach Angeline in his infamous striped sweater, exhorting the Tigers to give their all.

"Fran the Man"

F ran Angeline brought to the football-coaching job at U-E the same formidable focus that had set the founders, developers and kingpins of the village of Endicott apart from the rest of the crowd. Like Henry B. Endicott, George F. Johnson, Thomas J. Watson Sr., plastering and stuccoing giant Bill Gargano and others before and after him who have occupied positions of stature in Endicott, Angeline seized the moment. The early land barons, the manufacturers, the builders, the restaurateurs, the retailers, law-enforcement and firefighting and military personnel, members of the clergy, educational titans and governmental officials who catapulted the village to the summit all struck hard and fast. They helped shaped Endicott's destiny as a bastion. The impact of the coach who came to be known as "Fran the Man" was just as pervasive.

From his earliest days as the high school football coach in Endicott, Angeline demonstrated a personality that differentiated him from his counterparts in the profession. His coaching adversaries (Dick Hoover of Vestal, Cal Rucker of Susquehanna Valley, Hank Diller of Johnson City, Gordie O'Reilly and Jud Blanchard of Binghamton North, Bud Deyo of Binghamton Central, Tom Hurley of Elmira Southside, Joe Moresco of Ithaca, Bill Plimpton of Elmira Free Academy, et al) were equally dedicated and driven. They had other traits in common with Angeline as well. That didn't make Angeline any less of a rare commodity.

Angeline's seeming imperviousness to cold, for instance, quickly became something of a local legend in Endicott.

Fog and cold are standard in the autumn months in Endicott. Fog rolls in off the Susquehanna River late at night and lingers like a thick cloud long after the sun has come up. Once in the 1970's, driving my motorcycle home from work after helping put another edition of the Sunday sports section of the *Press & Sun-Bulletin* "to bed," I chanced upon two cats sitting about four or five feet apart near the middle of the road. I didn't see them until it was too late. They didn't budge as I split the space between them, uttering a startled "whoa" as I breezed past and continued on my way. They must have been as surprised as me; too surprised to move.

The same sort of fog made it an adventure whenever my cousin Clarence Fowler and I decided to play En-Joie Golf Club at the crack of dawn on the weekends. We'd try to ascertain "direction of flight" as our shots disappeared from the tee box into the wet haze, and then, our golf shoes soaked from the dew that lathered the fairways, grope around like a couple of blind men in an attempt to determine where the balls had come to rest.

"Endicott fog" makes all sorts of outdoor forays an exercise in recklessness.

The kind of cold that goes with living in "upstate" New York is a challenge too. From at least Halloween and sometimes well before the end of October, the temperature drops dramatically as evening arrives, going lower and lower—like a dexterous, flat-bellied dancer trying to slide under a limbo stick. As a sportswriter covering high school football games at night from press boxes that were open to the elements and that sat high above the field, like the ones at Vestal High and Binghamton North, I learned to live with—but never accept—the biting cold.

"Look at Angeline!" I shouted, nudging my buddies. "Just a sweater!" We were sitting directly below the press box on the U-E side of the field at Ty Cobb Stadium. In the early 60's, when he took over as U-E's football coach, no matter how far the reading on the thermometer plunged and even when rain or sleet or snow filled the black sky on Saturday nights, Angeline stalked the side-lines in front of the U-E bench with nothing more than a striped button-down sweater as protection from the chill and damp. It was the same whether the Tigers were playing at home or on the road. The elements appeared to have no visible effect on him, and he made no concession whatsoever to them. U-E fans became so used to seeing Angeline in shirtsleeves, or wearing just a hooded sweatshirt, on the foulest of nights, that watching him became a spectator sport. All eyes were riveted on him as he led the team onto the field; the crowd was like an audience waiting in anxious expectation for the start of a fashion show. Even when he got older and "graduated" to a three-quarter-length leather jacket, Angeline seldom if ever wore gloves. In all the years I followed my hometown team, I never knew him to put a hat on his head. When it got bitterly cold, U-E fans would break out the blankets and winter clothing; opposing coaches would revert to knit caps or lined trench coats. Angeline would be the lone wolf, standing in defiance of the opposing team—and Mother Nature.

During my sports-writing years, I noticed that Angeline was lib-eral in doling out nicknames for people. I became aware, too, that he did it not just as a means of identification. It was also a term of endearment. He never made a big deal about this practice in public, but it was important to him. Angeline's affection for the individuals who made up the U-E football family and the larger football fraternity was genuine; he showed his respect for them by personally coining, or rendering approval for, the "tag" these folks were given. The habit is a fairly common one in the military and in the world of sports; "Fran the Man" savored the chance to honor associates and friends in this manner, attaching a nickname to them as if he was an officer pinning medals on a deserving fellow soldier. The many U-E football players who acquired nicknames as they came through the program weren't the only ones singled out for recognition in this way; some coaching rivals, some opposing players, some U-E football assistants and some ardent supporters of "Tiger ball" were given shortened or colorful monikers too.

These nicknames ranged the gamut from the obvious and simple to the more obscure and complex. Those ascribed to three of Angeline's closest colleagues needed little explanation: former U-E Superintendent of Schools Richard McLean, who was "Mac;" former U-E Athletic Director Bob Wurtenburg, who was "Wurt;" and big Bob Adams, a U-E assistant coach, who was "Beef."

McLean, then retired and apparently already suffering from the ills that would take his life before the year was out, served as master of ceremonies at the farewell testimonial dinner for Angeline in February of '93 (similarly, McLean had chaired a salute to the coach on Angeline's twenty-five years of service to the village of Endicott, in the winter of 1984). Assistant Coach Bob "Beef" Adams was the first assistant coach hired for Angeline's staff at U-E back in 1960 and together with Dick "Hovie" Hover and Russ Nicosia became an early pillar of the U-E football program.

Opposing players, like Vestal's Dave Cook ("Cookie") were sometimes referred to by nicknames they had already been accorded, or acquired along the way. The most colorful and creative nicknames were reserved for those who wore the Orange and Black. Barry Doyle, a defensive corner in the mid-80's and one of the most vicious hitters ever to suit up for U-E, was "Oil Can" Doyle (maybe because after he laid foes out, they needed lubrication to get their joints moving again!). QB Rod Zur, known for his fluidity, was "The Glider." Tom Fiori, who had cool blue eyes, was "The Ice Man." Swarthy U-E equipment man Mike Fabrizio (a massive U-E lineman in his playing days) was "Magilla Gorilla." Superstar thrower/runner Ed Koban was "Fast Eddie" Koban. Dynamite blocker Joe Amorese was "Ammo." Halfback, basketball player and track triple jumper Jim Newfrock was "Frog." The greatest player I ever personally witnessed suit up for U-E, the swift and shifty Tom Bennett, was "Burnin' Ben" Bennett. Premier linebacker Dave Wolf was "The Wolf Man." Center/Noseman Todd Kehley, who stood six-foot-two and weighed two hundred fifty-five pounds, was "The Load." And so it went.

Like George F. Johnson, Angeline was an overachiever who placed great emphasis on meticulous preparation. Just as George F. had worked tirelessly to ensure that Endicott-Johnson continued to perform at peak efficiency, Angeline expended countless hours developing "Tiger ball" into a potent force. His absorption in the task was total. That left the job of running the Angeline household on the edge of Mersereau Park and the task of raising the Angelines' three children (Larry, Chris and Vaun) to Angeline's wife, Pat Angeline. A pretty, vivacious woman, Pat Angeline was as successful a wife, mother and homemaker as her husband was a coach.

The ever-present whistle dangling from his neck and the clipboard clasped in his left hand were two of the most conspicuous evidences of Angeline's commitment to his vocation. The clipboard became as lethal as a bayonet in his hand; he used it to diagram such innovations as the triple-option Wishbone attack, which U-E introduced in the fall of '74. Southpaw QB Tom "The Ice Man" Fiori was the triggerman in this new offensive scheme. The ploy proved more explosive than any formation the Tigers had unveiled to date. U-E averaged almost thirty-two points a game in compiling a 7-0-1 record that year, culminating in an 8-8 tie with Vestal. Fourteen thousand people showed up for that game!

The clipboard proved indispensable again twelve years later when the idea of a new formation, which the coaching staff dubbed "Top Gun," surfaced. It was unlike anything U-E opponents had ever faced: an unbalanced line to the left, filled with "prime beef."

It probably never occurred to Angeline, or anyone else, to draw parallels between George F. Johnson's contributions to the village, and Angeline's own. Still, Fran Angeline's impact on community life was enormous, and the influence he exerted on students, athletes and a host of others (inside and outside education) was felt for nearly as long in Endicott as Johnson's.

Endicott has been fortunate to have leaders like George F. Johnson and Fran Angeline.

None of them were better protectors of the public trust than Johnson. Angeline was cut from the same mold. As a Latin teacher, football coach and representative of the village's heritage and values, Angeline proved every bit as worthy of Endicotters' attention—and affection—as Johnson had.

Just as Johnson never let up in his plan to establish a model working community, Angeline never relented in his quest to build superior football teams at U-E.

Angeline and other Endicotters from every walk of life were able to pursue their dreams because of the environment Johnson had created, which encouraged experimentation and exploration.

From the moment George F. Johnson turned his eyes away from Leicestershire and pictured the sketchy outline of a new boot and shoe factory forming against the western horizon, Endicott's fate has been guided by single-minded men and women. With their bold strokes the founders—George F. Johnson, Henry B. Endicott and G. Tracey Rogers—had set in motion the construction of the fledgling village's first factory on a two hundred-acre parcel less than a mile north of the Susquehanna River and a few miles east of the already-established business district of neighboring Union. By that time—1900—downtown Union had a big head start on Endicott. Union's streets had been laid out and created around 1846. Three years later the New York and Erie Railroad came to Union; when the first train screeched to a stop at the new depot on North Street, a large crowd cheered. Around the same time, a bridge was erected over the Susquehanna River, replacing a ferry that had escorted horses and wagons from the north bank to the south bank. The bridge connected Union with an area that would become the town of Vestal.

By 1870, Union's compact inner core was already home to attorneys, justices of the peace, doctors, hotelkeepers, blacksmiths, a jeweler, a tailor, a newspaper editor, even a jailer. The lockup ("Fagan House," as it was called) was erected that year on Exchange Street. It was not the Taj Mahal; a log building, it consisted of two cells, each equipped with straw mats and board bunks. An unpretentious place, it nevertheless served the purpose.

Shortly after a blaze leveled virtually the entire south side of Main Street in 1874, Union formed a fire department. It added a school district in the mid-1800's.

Union was flourishing. Endicott hadn't yet emerged from its egg.

That would soon change, dramatically. With the erection of E-J's first factory on farmland Henry B. Endicott had purchased at the junction of Washington Avenue and North Street, Endicott began to take shape. Charles Wesley Harvey, a contractor, took charge of the operation. Men in wide-brimmed hats and suspenders, with pickaxes and shovels in hand, working side by side and in concert with plow horses, began the grading of Washington Avenue. The project took several years to finish. When they were done, The Avenue, although then just a dirt street, was a sight to behold, boasting all of the ingredients for success as a commercial zone: trolley tracks running down the center of the street; curbs; gutters and sidewalks; and shade trees on either side the entire length of the street.

These laborers also chiseled out Madison Avenue, North Street and, a few blocks east, McKinley Avenue.

The lure of the budding village of Endicott was irresistible. Shopkeepers led a wave of businesses to the street.

With the paving of The Avenue around 1920, more merchants arrived.

Coincidentally, it was in 1906, the same year the village of Endicott was incorporated, that Union received approval to operate a municipal lighting plant. Suddenly, both entities, Union and Endicott, had streetlights.

Washington Avenue, spurred by the influx of shoppers provided by Endicott-Johnson, became known as the place to purchase chocolate candy, a new suit or new dress, nuts and bolts, a wedding ring or a haircut. The Avenue grew and grew. Although it stretched only a few blocks in length, from Main Street on the southern end to North Street at its northern terminus, Washington Avenue seemed to attract every business under the sun. Before long there were seven restaurants on The Avenue and two saloons and a taxicab office and two theaters (the Ideal and the Lyric; the Ideal was subsequently replaced by the Strand, on the opposite side of the street).

By 1935, having weathered the years of the Depression, The Avenue had taken on a whole new look. Looking north from Main Street, one could see the same passageway, but many of the trees had disappeared, supplanted by wider sidewalks. Buses, not trolley cars, were now prevalent, as were automobiles, parked at angles on either side of the street. Rising against the sky at the northern end of The Avenue were the smokestacks of E-J's factories. Soaring upward, with the words "ENDICOTT JOHNSON" inscribed in capital letters on their exteriors from the top down, the smokestacks towered over the village's landscape, providing the citizenry with a sense of well-being.

The thousands of workers who poured out of the Johnson family's factories (and later Tom Watson's IBM plants) at noontime in pursuit of food, merchandise or services spawned the start of even more businesses, many of which, seeking unoccupied space, set up shop on North Street, just around the corner from The Avenue. Because of its handier proximity to "factory row," North Street quickly emerged as a perky commercial zone in its own right. Soon, E-J'ers and IBM'ers began patronizing such North Street businesses as Max Levenson's clothing store, Giordano's Barber Shop, Walters Laundry, the G.L.F. Cooperative and Moe's Cleaners. Many of these workers grabbed a bite to eat at the Sugar Bowl or Nick's Texas Hots. On steamy summer days during the 1950's I would pull my bicycle to a halt in front of Magic City Ice and Milk Co., on the north side of North Street a little west of the village center; there, I would obtain handfuls of ice chips from the big blocks of ice being broken up in front of the building. I would place them on my forehead or pop them into my mouth.

George F. Johnson was personally responsible for much of the growth that took place in Endicott in the first half of the twentieth century, but he put fairness—not rampant "progress"—at the top of his priority list. When it became apparent to Johnson in 1920, for instance, that a number of the village's merchants were charging E-J workers too much for eggs and milk and fruits and vegetables, he opened a farmer's market at the corner of North Street and McKinley Avenue. Local farmers, induced to participate by the offer of a small bonus, quickly embraced the concept. E-J workers, comforted by the knowledge that they would see set prices posted at the entrance to the market when they arrived for its opening at exactly ten o'clock in the morning, flocked to the site.

My Grandma Blossom, a farmer at heart, had a stall of her own at the farmer's market, where she sold homemade bread, cinnamon buns and other nourishments. She baked these in the kitchen of an apartment my grandparents lived in at the time, on North Street opposite Magic City Ice.

E-J also operated a company store on North Street, where customers could obtain groceries and other products.

It was into this atmosphere of thriving commercialism that Endicott's later giants joined George F. Johnson as shapers of the village's fortunes. When Fran Angeline arrived back on the scene in 1960, Endicott's luminance was already beginning to dull. His star, though, was on the rise. Still to come for him were the standout players, the gifted teams and the nonpareil seasons that would re-establish Endicott as a high school football steamroller.

Like George F. Johnson, Angeline adhered to the philosophy that, when it came to what could go wrong, "the devil was in the details." He overlooked no item, no matter how inconsequential it seemed. In his dealings with members of the media before and after games, he took special care to make sure they "got it right." He wasn't particularly trustful of their intentions. He went to extraordinary lengths (more than most of his coaching colleagues, it seemed) in an attempt to keep sportswriters "on track." After I became a sportswriter, this policy applied to me, even though I was a U-E grad and an unabashed admirer of Angeline-coached teams. My interviews with Angeline for the *Press & Sun-Bulletin's* popular "Monday Morning Quarterback" feature, in which area coaches "sounded off" in ad-lib, virtually unedited fashion on the game their teams had just played, and the one coming up, were invariably difficult affairs, punctuated by his assertions that the question I'd just asked was inappropriate, that there was too much of a focus on "the other guys" or that more emphasis needed to be given to a U-E player or an element of the Tigers' performance that had been overlooked. Because Triple Cities and Southern Tier coaches' comments for "Monday Morning Quarterback" ran virtually verbatim in the newspaper, and because their thoughts were occasionally incendiary ones, readers devoured the column as if they were Pac Man munching his way through a field of token interference.

Despite his protestations that the media sometimes got it wrong, Angeline was too big a man to blow off the scribes. Also, he knew newspaper coverage was essential in garnering the school the attention it deserved. When it came to sportswriters, he was always accommodating of his time. He was available at any hour of the day or night. This didn't mean the conversation would go smoothly. It seldom did, in fact. As a subject, he was a difficult interview: abrasive, argumentative, suspicious of the interrogator's motives. Although he tried hard not to "stir the pot" too intensely, his natural bent towards honesty produced observations for the "Monday Morning Quarterback" feature that jolted readers out of their seats. All of the coaches who participated used the forum as a foil to complain that the other team "ran up the score on us," that the officials "tagged us with too many unjustified penalties" or that "a bad break took our momentum away." For that reason, the column occasionally degenerated into a "pissing contest." Angeline and his colleagues even criticized the column from time to time for being too easy an invitation to trouble. The readers loved it, though. So did I.

In establishing himself as a luminary in Endicott during the second half of the 20th Century, Angeline enjoyed a huge audience. Shopkeepers, priests and nuns, factory workers, bus drivers and auto mechanics followed the exploits of the Orange and Black. Each week as the Tigers stormed into action on the road, or stampeded forth from their clubhouse at Ty Cobb Stadium, thousands cheered by way of encouragement. Countless more tuned into the games on the radio.

Through the 60's, 70's and 80's and into the 90's, as "Tiger ball" tightened its grip, the sight of the Orange and Black swarming at the edge of the gridiron caused foes' spines to curl in concern and sportswriters' eyebrows to lift in respect. U-E teams were like a small army marching toward glory. Angeline was the army's intrepid field general, exhorting his troops to play as if there was no tomorrow.

One detail Angeline never overlooked was the pronunciation of the names of the athletes he reported to the newspaper. Whether he was talking with a sportswriter about a U-E football player, or calling in the results of the village's summer-recreation youth tennis program, he insisted that each individual's name be spelled correctly in the newspaper the next day. He did this by pronouncing the name slowly in his familiar husky voice, breaking it into syllables so that there could be no mistaking how it "sounded." Then, if necessary, he would spell the name. This practice repeated itself over and over, regardless of how many times he'd done it before. He approached this task as if it was a matter of life or death. Each and every name rolled off his tongue as if he was being paid to make sure there was no misunderstanding. I can still hear him pronouncing the names: "Han-a-fin..." "Pav-lo-vich..." "Ned-bal-ski..." "Ver-u-to..." "Pa-nic-cia..." "Ma-lar-key..." "Bed-doe..."

I always thought that Angeline would have made a great public-address announcer. I could picture him sitting in the press box at Ty Cobb Stadium, the names of the players cascading from the speakers with unerring accuracy. Like Bob Shepherd—the New York Yankees' PA announcer and the most eloquent deliverer of the spoken word I have ever heard (it has been said that ballplayers yearn to play in Yankee Stadium just to hear themselves introduced by Bob Shepherd)—Angeline would have done his homework and never garbled the name of a player...friend or foe. It was a matter of principle and pride with him.

The '60 season had finished on a bright note with the lopsided triumph over EFA and the tough "Mudder's Day" victory over Binghamton Central. Angeline's coaching career at U-E was off to a promising start. "Tiger Ball" would, over the course of the next three decades, take its place among the attributes Endicott could list as its claim to fame: E-J shoes; IBM office equipment; spiedies from the North Side; pizza; carousels; En-Joie Park; Washington Avenue.

U-E football was entering its Golden Age. Unfortunately, the village of Endicott was walking into a dark tunnel from which there would be no escape.

"Henry," a carousel horse, handcarved by Alfred Eno of Endwell, New York and loaned to the Endicott Visitor Center for exhibit. The merry-go-round at West Endicott Park, one of a half dozen in the Triple Cities area, provided me with countless hours of enjoyment as a boy.

ROUND AND ROUND WE GO

A month past my fifteenth birthday, I was still enough of an innocent to think that life went on forever. I believed this even though it collided with everything I had learned from Grandma Blossom who, quoting from her favorite source of reference—the Bible—seldom failed, in conversation, to remind people that a notorious antichrist (Satan) and a terrible place (Hell) really did exist; and that certain persons, starting with my drinking, swearing, nicotine-addicted uncle, George Hallberg, who'd "bounced around" before meeting and marrying my Aunt Peg, were destined to end up in the inferno, there to suffer the torments of eternal damnation, unless they reformed their ways.

Uncle George had been a convenient target for Grandma Blossom when I was young, and she selected him over and over in her efforts to make the point that unrepentant "sinners," upon leaving this world, would never experience the bliss of passing through the pearly gates and walking streets paved with gold. "Only the saved can get to Heaven," she'd say. Uncle George didn't buy it. He was not only an unwilling potential convert, he seemed to delight in rousing my grandmother's indignation by engaging in exactly the sort of behavior she detested. Sunday afternoons after church (which he never attended), gathered around the broad, thick-topped, rectangular wooden dining-room table at my grandparents' home in Apalachin, or lying on the floor in front of the fireplace in the parlor following the meal, I would listen intently as Grandma Blossom berated Uncle George for his delinquent ways. "Ah, hooey!" he'd yell back. Sometimes, turning his eyes toward me, he'd wink, which I took as a signal from him that "we guys have to stick together;" invariably, however, sensing that what my grandmother said was the gospel truth, and noticing the flames from the crackling logs in the fireplace shooting ever higher, I'd inch my body a little farther away from the red-hot pit. Maybe it was just my imagination, but at such moments I had the distinct impression that my grandmother, sensing that her message was having an effect on me, if not my uncle, was smiling inside—privately pleased with her effectiveness as a faithful disciple of our Lord.

When I was young, my Uncle George and Aunt Peg packed up everything they owned and moved to California. This took Uncle George almost as far from my grandmother, I surmised, as the earth's surface would allow. Surprisingly, my grandparents, once they retired completely from their labors, followed suit, selling their house and shedding many of their possessions. As a result, in the most bizarre of ironies, my grandparents and my aunt and uncle and my cousin Richard Hallberg were suddenly reunited and living together under one roof! When I landed at my Aunt Peg's house in the fabled Franciscan-fathers' mission city of San Gabriel in 1966, after making the trip west with my uncle (Bernard Turner) and my friend Dan Murphy, nothing had changed. Grandma Blossom and Uncle George were still at opposite ends of the religious spectrum. Somehow, though, they were managing to co-exist in a reasonably non-contentious manner in a two-story house on a quiet residential side street.

Having been earmarked for a total-body immersion in the waters of the baptismal font at West Endicott Baptist Church as a youth, and with the "revelations" I'd received from Rev. John

Green during his tedious sermons—reinforced by the lessons I'd gotten from my Sunday School teachers and my grandmother—I should have known beyond a shadow of a doubt that life has a beginning and an ending. And yet there was evidence to the contrary: the merry-go-round at West Endicott Park spun round and round day and night, and my 45 RPM records did too.

The "action," it seemed, never stopped.

The merry-go-round at West Endicott Park was one of a number of colorful wooden carousels sprinkled like sunflowers in parks throughout the Triple Cities. At one time or another I rode all of them; the one in West Endicott more than any of the others, however. It was within easy walking distance of my grandparent Lees' house: east on Jennings, right onto Mills, left onto Maple. I rode it constantly, never tiring of the sense of rapture, the feeling of release, it provided.

My association with the carousel at West Endicott Park had begun when I was just a tot; my father would place me in the saddle of one of the horses and stand beside me as the carousel's operator, positioned in an open dirt spot in the middle of the ride, pulled a lever. Like magic, the scruffy floorboards would start to move and the Wurlitzer military band organ would begin to pump out rousing Calliope music. My mother would find a place outside the chain-link fence that surrounded the carousel to watch, and my father and I would wave to her each time the horses, rising and falling on the greased metal poles to which they were attached, made another complete revolution. Every time the music died and the merry-go-round ground to a stop, I'd ask my father, as if our very lives depended on his answer, "Can we go again?"

When I was about seven years old, my brothers and I would emerge from the wading pool at the far end of the park, purchase a Tootsie Pop from the snack bar and sprint to the merry-go-round. There, with towels wrapped around our waists to cover our soaking-wet bathing suits, we'd scramble to claim our favorite horse before someone else got hold of it. The most popular horse was actually part boar and part dog; our eyes would fix on its location as the previous ride stopped and never stray from it as we plotted the shortest route to get to the spot. When the gate was opened to let us in, there would be a mad dash of bodies; kids scrambled like scavengers in an effort to be "the first."

By the time I'd reached the ages of thirteen and fourteen, "my crowd," which included my cousin Jack and many of the park's regulars from West Endicott, practically ran West Endicott Park. In the summertime, we'd arrive early and stay all day, terrorizing the younger children as we moved from the tennis courts to the badminton nets to the swings. One minute we'd be hanging out in the covered pavilion. The next we'd be wrestling in the grass behind the slides or buying an ice cream bar or a creamsicle or Fireballs from the snack bar. We "owned" the park like Al Capone—"Public Enemy No. 1"—had owned Chicago.

By then, the crowd I ran with hailed primarily from Union and West Endicott and included Laurene Perfetti, Penny Chetko, Pat Steenburg, Josie Shady and others who lived nearby. By that time, too, I had mostly abandoned the merry-go-round's horses in favor of one of two baroque chariots that held up to six people each. In those seats, which featured high sides (making what transpired within the seats harder for nosy adults to detect), Perfetti and I kissed and touched for the first time…the start of a relationship that was soon burning out of control. Our "advances" on one another spilled over onto beach towels thrown down in quiet places in the park, to the darkened seats in the side aisles of the Elvin Theater, to the sidewalks leading from the Jennie F. Snapp School in Union to Laurene's house on Wilma Street in West Endicott and finally to her living room. There, alone in semi-darkness for an hour or more when her parents weren't home, our romantic urges erupted, virtually unchecked, on the sofa.

— ❖ —

Like the merry-go-round, my 45's removed all cares and worries. Listening to them reinforced my notion that life offered limitless possibilities, and that my teen years—punctuated by sock hops, soda shops, Topps baseball cards and model airplanes (which hung from the ceiling of my bedroom)—would last forever. Thanks to my regular trips to Woody's, on The Avenue, my collection of 45's rivaled anyone else's. The early voices of "doo wop," "Pop" and "Rock 'n' Roll" that exploded from the speaker of my turntable provided all the enticement a teenager hungry to experience new frontiers needed. From Pat Boone's "Love Letters in the Sand" to Elvis Presley's "Blue Suede Shoes" to The Coasters' "Yakety Yak" to The Everly Brothers' "Bye, Bye Love" to Bobby Rydell's "Wild One" to Little Anthony and the Imperials' "Tears On My Pillow" to the Chordettes' "Lollipop," to Danny & the Juniors' "At the Hop" to The Big Bopper's "Chantilly Lace" to Jan & Dean's "Baby Talk," I was in a perpetual state of expectation about the good times that were still to come.

Had someone suggested to me in the fall of 1960 that my village was beginning its inevitable disintegration and that differences were driving a wedge between members of my own family, I would have said, "That's absurd." And yet it was true. I didn't want to believe that the long naps my grandfather was taking on the porch swing were a sign of impending doom.

My family's own great run in the construction business was slowing to a trot. From around 1910 which is about when my grandfather started working as a tanner for E-J until the late 1960's when the shoemaking colossus began struggling to survive, the fortunes of E-J, the village and the Lee family had been close-ly linked. George F. Johnson had succeeded in creating the utopi-an community of "little pink houses" he'd envisioned. My uncle—Robert E. Charlesworth Stanton "Bob" Lee—through the launch of Lee Window Unit Co. and in collaboration with his brothers and associates like Sam Bevilacqua, Frank Ambrose, Bud Bogart and Chet Dearing—had provided windows, doors and later scores of homes for E-J and IBM workers and others as the greater Endicott area grew and prospered.

And then it was over.

Upon retiring from E-J at the age of sixty, my grandfather received a letter. Dated August 2nd, 1948, it was printed on Endicott-Johnson Corporation stationery with the company seal and the words "BETTER SHOES...FOR LESS MONEY" and "Endicott, N.Y.," gracing the top of the page. It was addressed to "Mr. Horace Lee/Upper Leather Tannery."

It read:

> Dear Mr. Lee:
>
> Wisdom comes only through years of experience. That is why we place so much value on older workers. You are anchors in the business, [who] teach uncertain ones and keep us from drifting in troublesome times.
>
> It is with sincere appreciation we present this certificate commemorating your long and helpful service with our company.
>
> Cordially,
> George F. Johnson
> George H. Johnson
> Charles F. Johnson Jr.

George F. Johnson died three months later, on November 28th, 1948. My grandfather would live on for another thirty-two years, passing away in Endicott on September 25th, 1980 at the age of ninety-two. My grandmother, Lillian B. (Stanton) Lee, died in Florida, where she was living with her eldest daughter, my Aunt

Harriet, at the time, on October 20th, 1981, at the age of ninety. Both are interred at Riverside Cemetery in Union. Several of my grandparents' deceased children, including my dad, are buried in Riverside Cemetery too.

Both of my grandparents had worked for E-J. A number of other family members had too, including my Uncle Bob, who started working for E-J as a shoemaker at the age of sixteen before establishing his own business. Because of George F. Johnson, my grandparents were able to escape the drafty shack in Orson, Pennsylvania in which they first lived as newlyweds (and where their fourth-born, Dora, succumbed to pneumonia at the age of one year and ten months) and come to Endicott to work for E-J and to acquire an E-J house. Because of Johnson, they were able to overcome the initial tragedies that beset them, like the death in the early to mid-1920's of first little Erwin and then his brother Charles Francis (both of whom passed away in Endicott), and my grandfather's apparent brief liaison with another woman. Because of Johnson, my grandparents were able to live out most of their final years in tranquil comfort—my grandfather spreading the sawdust he'd collected at my uncle's mill around his rose bushes, my grandmother baking sugar cookies in her small, warm kitchen at the back of the house. She'd give the cookies to her grandchildren at Christmas time, with a five-dollar bill inside the package. She also crocheted doilies, which she placed on plant stands and end tables and coffee tables around the house.

E-J'ers like my grandparents rode the shoulders of George F. Johnson to a better life. His broad shoulders carried them and a working force of thousands—indeed an entire village—forward. Because of George F. Johnson, Endicott would attain the fulfillment of its promise as "Shoe Town, U.S.A."

If only for all too short a time.

Bob Lee, my uncle; a skilled amateur boxer and founder of Lee Window Unit Co.

"I Prouda I Endicott"

By the early 1960's, the swing of the pendulum told the bittersweet tale: its downward plunge indicative of the village's imminent demise, its upswing reflective of U-E's reincarnation as a high-powered high school football locomotive.

The warning signs had begun to surface as early as 1948, the very year George F. Johnson passed away. On April 19th of that year, the famous octagon-shaped building known as the Casino—the cornerstone of Ideal Park (later En-Joie Park)—burned to the ground. Gone in clouds of smoke was the enchanted wood and stone structure; gone with it were the building's cigar and candy stands and soda fountain and popcorn booths. Removed from the scene was the structure in which Endicotters had gathered for concerts, minstrel shows, boxing matches, dancing and roller-skating. It would not be replaced.

Less than a year later, on March 21, 1949, the covered grandstand at the eastern end of the park, from which more than five thousand persons could watch horse racing, went up in flames. It too was gone for good.

The final blow came in the late 1960's when the park's by then-aged and dilapidated swimming pool was smashed to bits and the hole it occupied filled in. This, coupled with the dismantling of

En-Joie's merry-go-round, which was relocated to Highland Park in Endwell—now a continent away, for all intents and purposes—signified the end of En-Joie Park.

E-J had all but vanished. Now En-Joie Park was gone.

Not long after, my uncle's one-story cider-block mill on Jennings Street in West Endicott—Lee Window Unit Co.—caught fire. A fixture in West Endicott for almost fifty years, it was reduced to rubble. The spectacular blaze was the talk of the town. My uncle, who lived directly opposite the mill in an attractive, spacious two-story Colonial, dragged machines out of the ashes and had them cleaned, rewired and installed in a nearby rented building in an attempt to save his business. Despite his valiant effort, he could not keep things going for long. He was by then too old to jump-start the operation. The mill too was now gone. Many members of the Lee family had worked there, or been employed by my uncle's firm: my grandfather, after he retired from E-J; my mother, as the business's secretary; my father, as both a shop hand and a carpenter; my Uncle Ray; my Uncle Stew; my cousin Danny; another cousin on my dad's side, Joe Lee. Two men who were virtually "blood" by way of their long association with the Lees—Sam Bevilacqua and Frank Ambrose—had run the shop with aplomb for years. Whenever I walked onto the sawdust-splattered floor of the shop, I found Sam and Frank there—fixed objects, like the power saws scattered all about—a carpenter's pencil stuck behind one ear as they set panes of glass or angle-cut the corners of window frames.

Uncle Bob was either the brainiest of my grandparents' many children—or the shrewdest. I assumed—not completely incorrectly—that he was one of the most accomplished members of the merchant community West Endicott had ever produced. My uncle had built his business from scratch, just like West Endicott restaurateur Gregrio "Gree" Fusco. Gree Fusco and Bob Lee dominated their respective spheres of endeavor in West Endicott for a long time.

Gree Fusco was the first Italian immigrant to settle in what would become West Endicott; legend has it that it was Fusco who convinced George F. Johnson to choose the future West Endicott as the site of a "dream neighborhood" of factories, homes and parks when Johnson was ready to look for land to "grow" his burgeoning shoe and tanning venture beyond Endicott. They were good friends; soon after arriving in the United States, Fusco had gone to work for Johnson as a gardener and landscaper. Fusco supervised the planting of trees on the original Johnson homestead in Endicott. The two men remained friends even after Fusco ventured in another direction to launch a restaurant. Johnson trusted Fusco.

Upon Johnson's recommendation and possibly as a result of Fusco's influence, E-J purchased thirteen hundred acres of land just west of the village of Endicott, named the area West Endicott, and paid for the grading of wide streets and the installation of cement sidewalks, attractive boulevard lights, water and sewer. The company built ball diamonds. It built West Endicott Park. It was in West Endicott that my grandparents took up residence in an E-J house, to raise their family.

Gree and Mary Fusco's warm and cozy restaurant in a two-story block building on North Page Avenue in West Endicott was an institution when I was a kid; my family ate at Fusco's Beer Garden often.

Gree Fusco, Bob Lee and Roy Rosencrance (who operated Ideal Lanes, where all of the Lee men bowled on a regular basis) were big names in West Endicott during the early years of the neighborhood's existence.

The trappings of my uncle's personal success were not hard to find. They were abundant enough for me to appreciate: the low-slung but long and roomy commercial building in which his business was housed, taking up almost a whole corner of land in West Endicott; the spacious home he, my Aunt Alberta and their children—my cousins Sandra, Robert Lee Jr., Roberta ("Berbie") and Sharon—occupied; the big, expensive cars my uncle drove; the fact that, unlike my dad, he always had a wad of bills in his pocket. I'd heard my uncle was a good fighter during his boxing days; I accepted these stories on faith: even when he got older, he possessed the "bounce" one would recognize as a trademark quality of the man who could "bob" and "feint" and "jab" and "hook" with the best of them. I didn't need to "just believe" that he was an entrepreneurial Samson, either; I had seen the evidence first-hand.

When I did odd jobs around the house for my uncle, he always put at least a ten-dollar bill in my hand. At the ages of twelve and thirteen, this was quite a windfall to me, and I'd make a beeline for the candy store one block away to buy baseball cards, licorice and bubble gum.

When, as an adult, I needed the warped top of an antique library table planed prior to refinishing it, I took it to my uncle. "Sure!" he said, placing the stump of a cigar in the ash tray on his desk. The work was provided free of charge. Similarly, when, emulating my grandfather, I started using sawdust from the mill as mulch, I was allowed to take as much as I wanted.

Lee children were always welcome at the mill. I went there frequently in the 1950's, after school, to catch a ride home to West Corners from my mother, and would hang out with her in the office, or with Sam Bevilacqua and Frank Ambrose, in the shop. The door to my uncle's office was always open. Animated and outgoing, he enjoyed company, and loved to converse with guests.

My grandfather was the patriarch of the family, and its clown prince; my uncle was the closest we'd come to a tycoon. Between them, they commanded a good deal of attention.

With the loss of George F. Johnson, E-J, En-Joie Park and finally the shocking demise of The Avenue, the village of Endicott slid into a morass from which it never again fully emerged. Old-timers shook their heads in disappointment at the sight of their company town hitting the skids. The nervy among them pointed the finger of blame at the village itself: criticism for which there appeared to be ample justification. The village, after all, had leased and maintained En-Joie Park for several years starting in the late 1960's after E-J sold the grounds to the Union-Endicott School District. For En-Joie Park to fall into irreversible disrepair so rapidly and then to be abandoned altogether suggested to them that the village was a much poorer steward of the property than E-J. "This never would have happened if George F. Johnson was still alive!" they cried.

During the 1960's and 1970's, Endicott crumbled like a house of cards. In astonishing and disconcerting fashion many of the buildings and businesses that had grown up around E-J and that had fed off the company's success were erased from the landscape as if they had been mere jottings on a blackboard. Many of the village's institutions that fell into this category had been nurtured into fruition by E-J in the first place, bolstered financially by the company and finally given to the village at a bargain price or for no cost at all. One of these was George F. Johnson's home on Park Street, which became the George F. Johnson Memorial Library in November of 1950 after being sold to the village by Johnson's daughter, Lillian (Johnson) Sweet. The property was sold to the village for what the late historian James V. Fiori, in his book *A History of Endicott*, described as "a token price of $50,000." Although Mrs. Sweet helped keep the library going in memory of her father for a number of years, it was finally demolished— despite strong protests from locals—to make way for a new library on the same site. In a gesture that was characteristic of the Johnson family's unconditional love for the village of Endicott, Mrs. Sweet continued to support the library with donations of money and stock for years afterward.

I had spent my formative years frolicking in En-Joie Park, perusing the bookshelves at the George F. Johnson Memorial Library for sports tomes like *Hot Corner* (about a star high-school third baseman) and playing billiards and basketball at the first Endicott Boy's Club. Each of the three properties was worth its weight in gold—or so it had seemed before they were lost. En-Joie Park had been one of Endicott's longstanding treasures. George F. Johnson's home was no less special. It represented the most personal of the Johnson family's many gifts to the community when it became available for use as the village library. Likewise the first Endicott Boy's Club, on Broad Street, which was once the home of Mr. and Mrs. Chester B. Lord—prominent and civic-minded early citizens of the village. In 1930, the Lords opened a hospital—the Bradford Lord Memorial Hospital, for handicapped children—on the premises. They operated the hospital until 1944, when the hospital's functions were relocated to Binghamton. The Lord property was then summoned into action as the first Endicott Boy's Club. It served in that capacity until the early 1960's when a new Boy's Club (for boys and girls) was erected on the south side of East Main Street, near the river.

I spent countless boyhood hours at En-Joie Park, the George F. Johnson Memorial Library and the first Endicott Boy's Club. The loss of these properties left a void that would never be filled.

As homemakers, my mother and my friend Huey Boyle's mom (Morey Boyle) had taken Huey and I to En-Joie Park often. There, we'd drift lazily through the cool, shaded grounds, set up lunch on a picnic table or play pinball games in the enclosed pavilion. When I was old enough, I was sent to En-Joie for swimming lessons in the shallow end of the pool. My teeth chattered upon entering the frigid waters early every Saturday morning. Once I was proficient enough to hold my own at the larger depths, I swam at En-Joie for years with my brothers and my friends. I became adept at "ducking" the cold shower swimmers were subjected to as they passed into the pool through the entrance to the big bathhouse. Unfortunately, En-Joie Park itself couldn't "duck" the doom that was its fate.

En-Joie Park had been developed in the late 1800's to promote travel on the Binghamton, Lestershire and Union Railway and by trolley car. It once boasted such amenities as a bicycle track, the Casino, lagoons, rustic bridges, shaded seats and paths, bandstands, tennis courts, a race track, a covered grandstand, horse stables, boathouse buildings and of course the pool. All of these disappeared piece by piece until nothing was left.

In the years following these setbacks, The Avenue all but died as one store and one business after another took leave of its premises.

The spotlight shifted. The glory that Endicott would attain over the next three decades was provided not exclusively by E-J, IBM and The Avenue but also by the football teams assembled by Fran Angeline. The milestone days and nights—almost all totally deserving of replay—slowly but surely began to materialize for my alma mater, starting with the first of what Angeline would later refer to as U-E's many "barnburners" against Vestal: a 13-0 Bears' victory at U-E in '62 before a crowd of 13,000. That night's game was marked by touted Vestal sophomore Bobby Campbell's tremendous performance as a "triple-threat" back. Campbell went on to star for Coach Joe Paterno at Penn State and was drafted by the NFL's Pittsburgh Steelers. Following their shutout win over U-E that evening in '62, Vestal fans "rubbed it in" by driving through the streets of Endicott—their car horns blaring announcement of the outcome.

Under Angeline, U-E, like E-J, would produce its share of "Kodak moments" for Endicott to embrace. There were all of the following and more to savor in the years to come:

- The unveiling of U-E's infamous "racehorse," or "quick-huddle," offense;

- U-E's first Southern Tier Conference (STC) title in 1964, the securing of which was led by John "The Plow" Blishak and Mickey Murtha. The '64 season culminated

with the Tigers' 13-13 tie against Vestal before a crowd
of nearly 17,000 in a battle of 7-0-0 and 6-0-1 squads;

- Angeline's "breakthrough" victory over the Bears, 20-12, in 1965;

- The installation of the triple-option ("Wishbone") attack in '74, which produced a 7-0-1 season that ended with another momentous tie against Vestal (8-8);

- A 51-yard-plus field goal by Ron "The Bionic Man" Rejda at Newburgh in '76;

- The undefeated '79 season;

- A political "pep-rally" visit to Ty Cobb Stadium by President Reagan in '84, for which Angeline and his Tigers were provided with a "ringside" seat;

- The introduction of the "Top Gun" offense and the Tigers' victory over Binghamton North in '86 that snapped the Indians' 21-game winning streak;

- The 11-0 record of '89 when the Tigers finished No. 1 in the Southern Tier Athletic Conference (STAC), No. 1 in the state and No. 19 in the nation (according to USA Today).

The 1900's were "Endicott's century." The arrival of Henry B. Endicott and George F. Johnson, the mapping of streets and blocks, the establishment of E-J's factories, the evolution of Washington Avenue, the incorporation of the village in 1906 and the emergence of IBM—"Big Blue"—pushed Endicott to the forefront. Then along came Fran Angeline and the speedy and explosive Union-Endicott High School football teams of the later years of the century to add an exhilarating new chapter to the village's history.

And then the merry-go-round came to a stop—figuratively if not literally.

Today, longtime residents of Endicott who experienced any part of the village's golden years are filled with nostalgia and regret. They yearn for a return of the good old days, when E-J's smoke-stacks rose high above North Street and when Washington Avenue flourished. They are not unappreciative, however. They can still say that once upon a time, Endicott was the greatest shoe town of them all.

Words an elderly Italian gentleman spoke as he took Fran Angeline's hand in his during a chance crossing of their paths on Washington Avenue just after the Tigers had completed their fan-tastic '89 season sum up how immigrant and native-born residents of Endicott alike feel about their football and their village:

"Coach, tanka you team very much for whata you do for all…I prouda I Endicott."

Three generations of Angelines about to enter "Fran Angeline Field
House" at Ty Cobb Stadium for a little workout in the Summer of '02.
From the left, Chris Angeline's sons Cary and Ryley, "Grandpa" Fran,
Larry Angeline (holding his son Andre) and Chris Angeline.

"WHICH WAY E-J?"

For a little while on a weekday afternoon in September of 1984, U-E High School's Ty Cobb Stadium was transformed from a football field into a political arena. Standing at a podium on a platform placed near the stadium's eastern end zone—looking boyishly handsome for a man of sixty-eight years in the glint of the sun sinking toward the horizon over the Susquehanna River, behind him—was the fortieth president of the United States of America: Ronald Reagan.

A visit to a remote outpost like Endicott by any commander in chief, Democrat or Republican, is a rare occurrence. This was Reagan's first and only such trip to "the very center of your beautiful 'Valley of Opportunity,' " as he put it in his opening remarks. Excitement over the president's appearance had been building since the word went out in the dog days of August that he would be coming to Endicott. It was now ready to erupt in affectionate embrace, exactly as his re-election team, driving hard for a second term for the Reagan-Bush (George Herman Walker Bush) administration, had planned. Long before wristwatches reached 4:34 P.M., signaling the time for the start of the president's address, most of the 25,000 persons in attendance had passed through the heavily guarded entrances to Ty Cobb Stadium with their miniature American flags and binoculars in hand and taken their places in the bleachers. They were ready. It was one of the largest throngs ever assembled for an event—sporting or otherwise—in the history of the stadium.

The atmosphere for the occasion was unlike any residents of Endicott had experienced. Security and communications personnel had taken over the field house days earlier, forcing Coach Angeline and his football team to use an alternate locker room to suit up for practice sessions in preparation for their '84 season opener at Liverpool (near Syracuse). At the rally itself, Secret Service agents, their penetrating and unforgiving eyes probing every face for the slightest hint that a potential assassin (like a future John Hinckley) had infiltrated the gathering, ran interference as Reagan moved among the multitude. Sharpshooters stood on the roof of the high school, armed to the teeth. Rumor had it that submarines were trolling the river in search of bombs or hit men! The president's own demeanor offered a striking contrast to that of his guardians. His lips and chin were creased in delight as he entered to a warm reception. The cufflinks on his white shirt gleamed. His dark, speckled tie was tied snug to his neck—a sign that his energy for the task of campaigning and for spreading his mantra of "peace through strength and economic growth through tax cuts" had not waned. He waved triumphantly in appreciation of the shouts of encouragement that pierced the air.

The entire U-E football squad, in full uniform, was accorded the privilege of sitting "front and center" for the speech. The team's captain, Maurice LaFuze, was chosen to walk on stage and present the president with a football jersey. Emblazoned on the jersey LaFuze handed President Reagan were the words "The Gipper-Number One," a bow to Reagan's portrayal of Notre Dame football player George "The Gipper" Gipp in the 1940 film *Knute Rockne All American*—about the legendary football coach.

— ❖ —

In his talk in Endicott that day, Reagan's voice seemed to choke a bit when he acknowledged knowing that "this valley holds a special story"—of "hardship overcome, of determination, hard work, family and faith." In many ways, he told his listeners, the story of Endicott's rise to greatness as a shoe town and a manufacturing juggernaut "is America's story." Endicott's legacy started, he pointed out, when George F. Johnson came to town to establish the community's first shoe factory. Thousands of immigrants, eager for work with the Endicott-Johnson Corporation, followed, he noted. Workers "came here with few possessions, many with nothing but the clothes on their backs. And they asked only (for) the chance to work, and work they did—long, hard hours tanning hides, cutting leather, stitching together the finished shoes. And as family helped family and neighbor helped neighbor, schools were built, houses were constructed, churches and synagogues were established. And this valley became home to some of the proudest communities in our nation, towns that had seen first-hand all that free men and women can accomplish."

Sitting in the bleachers directly above Reagan with my children and other members of my family by my side as the president's speech took shape, it was easy to identify with his words. Grampa Lee had put in more than three decades with Endicott-Johnson in the Upper Leather Tannery, or "hide house," in Endicott; my grandmother had worked in the Fair Play Factory on Page Avenue in West Endicott, not far from my grandparents' E-J house, helping produce men's and women's welt shoes.

When the shoe business "changed," ultimately forcing E-J to close its factories and tanneries and threatening the region's hard-won prosperity, IBM, which had been founded by Thomas J. Watson Sr., stepped up to "launch a revolution" that would change the world, Reagan said.

Growing up in the small town of Painted Post, New York—near Elmira—Watson "learned how to stick with a job until it is finished," Reagan said. "Watson started with a company whose mainstays were punch-card machines and time clocks (International Time Recording Co.)." In 1953, Reagan said, "the company that Watson had renamed IBM began making the first mass-produced commercial computer in history—the '650'—less than a half a mile from this spot."

Many of IBM's workers, he continued, "were sons and daughters of immigrants who had worked in the shoe factories. When they began, the best market researchers predicted that fewer than one thousand computers would be sold in the 20th Century. Well, IBM's first model sold almost twice that number in just five years, and now there are IBM plants in Endicott and around the world. And the computer revolution that so many of you helped to start promises to change life on earth more profoundly than the Industrial Revolution of a century ago."

Reagan's voice, clear and strong, resounded across Ty Cobb Stadium. "Already," he continued, "computers have made possible dazzling medical breakthroughs that will enable us all to live longer, healthier and fuller lives. Computers are helping to make our basic industries, like steel and autos, more efficient and better able to compete in the world market. And computers manufactured at IBM Owego, where some of you work, guide our space shuttles on their historic missions. You are the people who are making America a rocket of hope, shooting to the stars."

The lesson of the "Valley of Opportunity," Reagan said in summation, alluding to the accomplishments of men like George F. Johnson, Thomas J. Watson Sr. and Edwin Link (who developed the flight simulator and for whom the airport in Broome County is named), "is a lesson for our entire nation: with opportunity, there's no limit to what Americans can achieve."

— ❖ —

That Reagan's appearance was in part a ploy for votes became apparent when, in lauding the "vast economic expansion" the country had realized during the first four years of his watch, he asked members of the audience to take "a test." The answer to each question, he said, by way of obvious hint, would consist of three letters, the first two of which "are U.S." To each of the queries from the president that followed came the same thunderous response: "U.S.A.!" It came when he asked, "…of all the great industrialized nations in the world, which has shown by far the strongest, most widespread and most sustained economic growth?" It came when he asked, "[which] nation is showing the fastest rate of business investment in four decades?" And when he asked, "What country can say that its productivity is up, its consumer spending is up and its take-home pay is up?"

When the words "U.S.A." reached his ears for the last time, Reagan applauded his audience, telling his "students," "you scored 100!"

Watching the president, I felt nostalgic for "the old days." My grandfather had died almost exactly four years before—in September of 1980, at the age of ninety-two. My grandmother had passed away in October of 1981, at the age of ninety. Their former home on Jennings Street in West Endicott was no longer a rendezvous point for family gatherings. E-J's presence had been diminished substantially. Washington Avenue had given way as a shopping destination to the Oakdale Mall, in Johnson City, and to other more alluring retail magnets—like the new Boscov's department store, in downtown Binghamton, and stores and plazas along the Vestal Parkway in Vestal. The places around Endicott that had been beehives of activity in my youth—En-Joie Park, the Hotel Frederick, the first Endicott Boy's Club, the *Endicott Daily Bulletin* building, the Endicott-Johnson Corp.'s Endicott Restaurant, North Street Medical, the Strand Theater, the Neisner's, Newberry's and Woolworth's five and dime stores—had been erased from the landscape or were closed, never to reappear.

Some of the village's coaching legends had faded from view too; individuals I had glimpsed or come into contact with as a boy:

men like Harold V. "Ty" Cobb and C. Burdette Parkhurst. Burned into my memory were images of "Parky," a larger-than-life presence in the U-E boys locker room and the gymnasium and on the athletic fields when I first arrived at the high school. Parky even had an outdoor track meet named after him that I had covered as a sportswriter for the *Press & Sun-Bulletin*: the Parkhurst Invitational.

President Reagan might not have been privy to all of the details of U-E High School's rich athletic history—written so brilliantly by coaching giants like "Ty" Cobb, C. Burdette Parkhurst and Fran Angeline. Surrounded that day by local political cronies like the village of Endicott's first female public official—Mayor Marion Corino, whom he identified as "a proud Italian-American"—Reagan was certainly well aware of Endicott's meteoric rise to greatness as a factory town...a company town...a shoe town. Having toured the IBM Systems Technology Division facility—where he was briefed on computer production and final product assembly—before his speech, he closed his remarks by observing, "My dream for America, and I know it's one you share, is to see the kind of success stories in this valley multiplied a million times over."

Three different times during his speech, Reagan employed an expression he must have known—because of its self-explanatory implications—would tug at the hearts of many of those in attendance; and even generate a few tears. By 1984, most of Endicott-Johnson Corp.'s factories and tanneries were long gone from Endicott. Few vestiges of "the E-J years" were left. One of the scattered and treasured remnants was the very expression Reagan used that day—a simple and yet potent phrase that continues to affirm that, once upon a time, E-J—and Endicott—were synonymous with soaring success.

In using the expression, Reagan demonstrated he understood completely—and harbored a deep reverence for—what E-J's enormous influence had meant to the evolution of Endicott and "the Valley of Opportunity." He first used it to describe, perhaps somewhat tongue in cheek, the message he had instructed to be "radioed down" to the pilot of Air Force One when the craft got "a little off course" on its way into Link Field. At two other junctures in the speech he employed the expression again in tribute to the tremendous attraction George F. Johnson's company had for people who'd heard about Endicott-Johnson in their hamlets in distant lands.

As Endicott-Johnson emerged and its impact mushroomed, Reagan said, "Word spread all the way to Europe, and when immigrants from Poland, Russia, Czechoslovakia and a dozen other countries reached America's shores, thousands of them are said to have asked the way to this 'Valley of Opportunity' in the only English they knew:

"Which way E-J?"

The George F. Johnson statue in Endicott.

EPILOGUE

Was it all just a dream?

Did a man named George F. Johnson ever really exist, or was he a figment of a village's imagination?

Is it possible for any one person to have possessed such a colossal spirit? To have had the streets of Endicott and Johnson City paved at his own expense? To have introduced an eight-hour workday for his employees (in 1916, without a wage reduction) and, three years later, to bring forth profit-sharing? To have provided every newborn baby of E-J workers with a bank book indicating that a ten-dollar deposit had been made in the infant's name? To have provided the same child with a free pair of shoes? To have given his employees one-hundred percent medical, dental and hospital services at no charge to them? To have dug deeply into his own pockets to create public markets at which food was sold at prices E-J workers could afford? To have built thousands of homes that were made available to E-J workers at cost? To have donated millions of dollars to charitable causes? To have furnished free libraries, free parks and free amusements—including Broome County's famous carousels—for the benefit of not just E-J workers but an entire community?

Man, or myth?

From time to time over the years, critics and cynics have raised their voices to suggest that George F. Johnson was an opportunist, a conniver, an aberration. And to assert that E-J's seeming good will toward those in its employ amounted to nothing more than a self-serving paternalistic ploy: a gambit to keep workers "in their place." In the opinion of these stone throwers (who were few in number), the Johnson family's and E-J's corporate philosophy of a "square deal" for all masked a more devious plan: a desire to stamp out trouble (dissatisfaction, dissension, even outright labor unheaval) before it started. E-J's approach, in their view, was one of the oldest tricks in the book: bait the common folk with inducements; put enough "benefits" on the table (the thinking went) and you have "the rabble" hooked.

Nancy Grey Osterud, in an essay entitled *Working Lives* that was published by Binghamton's Roberson Center for the Arts and Sciences in 1982, contended that Johnson's practice of paying E-J employees on a piecework basis did not sit well with many E-J'ers. Osterud further asserted that E-J's "corporate-welfare measures" were designed to keep labor costs low and labor unions out. Johnson's "handouts" were a ruse to camouflage less-than-ideal working conditions, Osterud said; only by "separating" their "working lives" from their "private lives" could E-J workers accept this arrangement, she said. Their acquiescence was not an endorsement of E-J's methodology so much as it was a willingness to tolerate the status quo rather than risk losing everything, Osterud surmised.

This reasoning, of course, ignores reams of documentation (newspaper articles, photographs of Johnson co-mingling with his employees, letters George F. wrote to his workers, statements E-J workers have made about E-J, the erection of the famous arch in George F.'s honor by the workers themselves) that draw a far different picture; a picture of a company that valued its workforce as if it was family.

In May of 1993, Alice Rose Barnes of Vestal, in an interview with the *Press & Sun-Bulletin*, said, of Endicott-Johnson, "It was everything. I don't think there could be another company on earth as wonderful as that company was." Back in the 1920's, Barnes had enjoyed a five-year run as "Miss E-J," a role for which she'd been chosen based on her good looks, intelligence and character. As "Miss E-J," she went around meeting with workers, raising money for the poor and appearing in company magic shows.

Unlike Nancy Grey Osterud, Steve Hambalek—a long-time Binghamton-area newspaperman and a keen observor of goings-on in the Triple Cities who might have been expected to "see through" E-J's philosophical path if it was indeed a sham—instead came to the conclusion that Johnson was a miracle worker. Even with his discerning eye for carpetbaggers, shills and potion peddlers, Hambalek never doubted George F. Johnson's sincerity—or Endicott-Johnson's good intentions.

Hambalek may have put it better than anyone else has when, in evaulating Johnson's brilliant climb to stardom in the shoe industry, he wrote: "Johnson literally made the bootstraps by which he lifted himself from factory foreman to a partnership with Boston nobleman Henry B. Endicott."

The New York Times—arguably America's most respected newspaper—saw George F. Johnson's life and career the same way as Hambalek. When Johnson died in his home on Park Street in Endicott on November 28th, 1948—a little more than a month after observing his ninety-first birthday—*The Times*, in a front-page headline, announced:

G.F. JOHSON DIES;
HEADED SHOE FIRM
CHAIRMAN OF ENDICOTT-JOHNSON
CORP., 91, KNOWN FOR MANY
BENEFACTIONS TO WORKERS

The Times devoted the next seventeen inches of space to the accomplishments of George F. Johnson. The story was accompanied by a late-life photograph of Johnson—looking accommodating, patient and even saintly in his horn-rimmed glasses.

The Times identified Johnson as chairman of the board of "the second-largest shoe-manufacuring firm in the United States." Not once, in recharting Johnson's course from his first job as a treer in a boot shop in a small town in his native Massachusetts to the presidency of the Endicott-Johnson Corp., did *The Times* infer that Johnson was anything less than a godsend to the village of Endicott. On the contrary; the last portions of the article were devoted to Johnson's many heroic gestures; like the time he gave $150,000 to the city of Binghamton for development of a park site. He also paid for the equipment needed to outfit the park. Another time, when hundreds of E-J workers showed up at his doorstep to thank him for building a carousel at Endicott's North Side Park, Johnson smiled in humble gratitude and said "order anything you want from the concession stand at the park; put it on my tab."

Were these the overtures of a man with a dark ulterior motive? Or were they simply Johnson's way of reinforcing in the minds of E-J workers his oft-enunciated conviction that management and labor could accomplish more working harmoniously and in sync than they could in an atmosphere altered by the prospectively disruptive influence of an "organized" union? Present and future generations of Endicotters, historians and others must decide the answer to those questions for themselves. The evidence, however, overwhelmingly tilts in favor of the argument that George F. Johnson's numerous kindnesses toward his workers and the community at large came straight from a tender heart.

Much has been made of the fact that E-J workers never did form a collective-bargaining unit. There were repeated pressures to do so. Instead of giving in to the temptations cast before them on this matter, E-J workers "held fast to that which is good." Their loyalty to George F. Johnson, and to E-J, was absolute. In 1940, after E-J's employees resoundingly rejected a call for union representation in a National Labor Relations Board (NLRB) election, thousands of E-J'ers—an obviously happy lot—danced in the streets, held informal parades and staged a rally in front of George F. Johnson's home. What a lift that moment must have been for Johnson—then eighty-two years old and recovering from pneumonia!

In his interventions on behalf of the village, Johnson can even be credited with "saving IBM" for Endicott. Once, in a speech, Thomas J. Watson Sr.—founder of IBM—publicly thanked George F. Johnson for talking him out of moving the firm to another locale. Watson said Johnson told him, "Stay here in Endicott; skilled labor will come to you."

My life, growing up in Endicott in the 1950's and 1960's, was dominated by "the three F's:" family; factories; and football. Though by then deceased, George F. Johnson had made the emergence of "the three F's"—and so much more—possible. By creating E-J and by playing a prominent role in the founding and evolution of Endicott, he had provided jobs and an "E-J house" for my paternal grandparents—and churches, parks, playgrounds, medical facilities and schools for an entire populace, as the village took shape. By helping to launch the village of Endicott in the first place, he had set in motion the opening, in the early 1900's, of Union-Endicott High School—and the ensuing arrival at U-E of hundreds of standout football players. These sturdy sons of immigrants would proceed to make U-E football teams a force to be reckoned with on the gridirons of the Empire State—ensuring that "the Orange and Black" would be respected (and, frequently, feared) from the shores of Lake Erie to the lower reaches of the Hudson River and from the snowy fields of Onondaga County to the hardscrabble border cities and towns of northeastern Pennsylvania.

By establishing Washington Avenue/North Street area as the commercial center of the then-fledging village of Endicott, Johnson also inspired dozens of entrepreneruial-minded people to launch businesses. E-J, IBM and the village grew and prospered together, drawing strength from one another—like three tired and thirsty comrades drinking from the same well.

By the time I began my sophomore year at Union-Endicott High School in 1960, E-J was already beginning its inexorable slide down the mountain toward certain disaster. Then oblivious of anything unrelated to the world of sports, I had no clue that the end of the E-J era in Endicott was near—or that with E-J's demise would come the disintegration of The Avenue. Within a few years many of the pearls George F. Johnson and E-J had created for the enjoyment of all would fall: Johnson Field in Johnson City, home of the minor-league Binghamton Triplets; George F. Johnson's home-turned-library in Endicott; En-Joie Park in Endicott; the "CFJ" (for C. Fred Johnson) Pool in Johnson City (one of the first above-ground pools in the country, it could accommodate two thousand people). All of these were allowed to be plowed under or closed down despite vehement objections from members of the community.

Endicott almost lost its most beloved treasure too, with the revelation of a plan to demolish the arch on Main Street that E-J workers had paid for with their own money as a tribute to the company's—and the village's—guiding light: George F. Johnson. Mary V. Loomis, my dear old homeroom teacher at Jennie F. Snapp Junior High School, was one of those who refused to stand by and let it happen. "Endicott history should be saved," Mrs. Loomis huffed in a letter to the editor of the local newspaper. With the shadow of the wrecking ball looming literally within inches of the magnificent monument, a muncipal department head—Gene Kirdgus—stepped forward, in July of 1987, to present a design that called for "widening" the arch and thus improving traffic flow. Thanks to hundreds of loyalists like Mary V. Loomis who understood its significance, the arch was preserved. It still stands today. The very contemplation of the destruction of this precious symbol of Endicott's glory years makes my temperature rise. One afternoon in the summer of 2003, gazing at the beautiful statue of George F. that stands a short distance from the arch while on a visit home, I could almost hear him whisper, in his contemplations of the assets that Endicott has let go: "No! No! No!"

Between the early 1960's and the late 1990's, the Endicott-Johnson Corp. would experience a gradual "fade to black." During the late 1950's and 1960's, there had been unsuccessful takeover attempts—including one by the Glen Alden Corp., whose leaders acknowledged that they would have liquidated E-J. There were other warning signs. In 1961, speaking at a dinner of retired E-J workers, E-J President Frank A. Johnson said: "If we do not show progress in the coming year, there's no telling what will happen at the annual meeting in 1962." Abolition of the company's free medical program was a distinct possibility, he said.

By the time Frank A. Johnson delivered his dire message, the handwriting was on the wall. E-J's "numbers" had declined steadily from an earnings peak, in 1955, of $3.15 a share, to a loss—by 1961—of $2.22 a share. The company that had enjoyed its own page, for "E-J news" (retirements, longevity announcements, etc.), in the *Sun-Bulletin*, a Binghamton newspaper, was now gasping for air. By 1962 that very newspaper's Keith George, reporting on the outcome of an E-J stockholders' meeting, revealed the awful truth: E-J's workforce was down to twelve thousand and shrinking fast. Leaner days lay ahead, concluded Hammer & Co. Associates. In a study Hammer & Co. Associates undertook of the economic future of Broome County, it projected that E-J's ranks would be stripped to seven thousand workers by 1980. E-J's losses were piling up, the study said: E-J had run about one and a half million dollars in the red in 1960—and more than twelve million in the red in 1961!

Unless E-J implemented radical adjustments, it would be unable to compete with Genesco, International and Brown Shoe—"and more specialized shoe manufacturers," Hammer & Co. Associates asserted.

Therein lay the problem, industry experts said; in the face of a growing emphasis on "high fashion" footwear, E-J "mistakenly" primarily stuck to its "plain and simple working shoes."

In one column he wrote for the *Binghamton Press*, Steve Hambalek revealed that E-J's brass was "tossing overboard" everything not needed in the tight circumstances in which it was ensnared to save a sinking ship. Included in the deck-clearing, Hambalek said, were those workers, even members of upper management, who "couldn't or wouldn't adapt to the new order." There would be no further "forgiving," either, Hambalek said, of "incompetence, carelessness, malingering, waste" and "even thievery" as was the case in "the good old days."

Shortly after issuing his own red-flag remarks to retired E-J workers, Frank A. Johnson turned the reins of the company over to P.J. Casella. A Johnson-family member had been chief executive of E-J for the first eighty years of its existence; now it was time for someone else to lead. Nothing, however, could alter the inevitable. E-J would eventually be acquired by British-based Hanson Industries and then by U.S. Industries—owner of Jacuzzi, Ames garden tools, Ertl toys and Rexair vacuum cleaners. U.S. Industries kept the E-J name going by creating an "E-J footwear division."

The fate of E-J in Endicott and the Triple Cities was sealed, despite earnest efforts to keep the operation breathing. In 1992, the last of E-J's remaining plants in its onetime bastion of Johnson City—the E-J Rubber Division—was closed. In 1995, the last two of E-J's retail stores—one in Johnson City, one north of

Syracuse—closed (once, E-J had boasted more than two hundred such stores in thirty states). In February of 1998, U.S. Industries entered into a merger agreement with Zurn Industries; two months later came the announcement of the imminent shutdown of E-J's last plant: in Glendale, a few miles west of Endicott.

A one hundred six-year legacy had come to an end.

The stories linger. There are the ones about how, in the 1920's and 1930's, E-J workers would assemble a parade "at the drop of a hat." There are the ones about how IBM'ers came to E-J dinners and took one-dollar chicken or ham meals home with them to eat all week. There are the ones about how, during the Depression of the 1930's, George F. Johnson offered unemployed persons two "square meals" a day (breakfast and supper); hundreds of out-of-work persons jumped on freight trains to take Johnson up on his offer—many stayed on in Endicott for years. There are the ones told by former customers of E-J like Lucille Frechette, who remembered a time when buying E-J shoes was a ritual; it was a given that one would purchase a new pair of E-J shoes before returning to school in the fall or before starting a new job—or in anticipation of holidays, birthday parties, weddings, funerals and other milestones. In Lucille Frechette's case, it was patent-leather slingbacks with spiked heels and a bow; she bought them in Burlington, Vermont, for her honeymoon.

George F. Johnson is dead. E-J is gone.

All that's left are the memories. And the stories.

But, my oh my, what memories! And what stories!

INDEX

Abbott, Bud: 102

Adams, Bob "Beef": 95, 190

Adamson, Dave: 96

Agone, Robert D.: 33, 175

Albrecht, Jerry: 175

Alexander, Alex: 51

Allen, Mel: 77, 184

Allen, Steve: 111

Ambrose, Frank: 120, 206, 210, 212

Ameche, Alan: 54

Amorese, Joe: 191

Amos and Andy: 102

Anderson, Al: 142

Anderson, "Tank": 96

Angeline, Chris: 79, 156, 191, 218

Angeline, Francis J. "Fran the Man":
    18, 20, 33-34, 44, 56, 78-79, 82,
    91-92, 95-99, 103-104, 114-115,
    121-123, 127, 129-135, 139, 141-
    145, 152, 154, 156, 161-165, 169-
    170, 178-179, 181-192, 196-199,
    215-220, 224

Angeline, Larry: 191, 218

Angeline, Pat (Hanley): 191

Angeline, Vaun: 182, 183, 191

Apolovich, Alex: 111

Atkinson, Bobby: 60, 91, 122, 127,
    130, 138, 145, 164, 179

Atlas, Charles: 77

Avalon, Frankie: 125

Bacon, Louis: 107

Baker, Bill: 115, 122

Banks, Ernie: 101

Barber, "Red": 77, 184

Barno, Robert "Bob": 134, 175

Barton, Kirk "Corky": 95

Battaglini, Vic: 122

Battisti, Maurice F.: 153

Beach, Janet: 175

Beach, Mr.: 89

Becker, John: 171

Beddoe, Gary: 96

Beers, Matt: 96

Belardinelli, Dennis: 96

Bennett, Anne: 95

Bennett, Jim: 95

Bennett, Tom: 96, 191

Benny, Jack: 102

Berra, Yogi: 77, 79, 100

Berry, Chuck: 112

Best, Dave: 130-131, 150

Bevilacqua, Sam: 120, 206, 210, 212

Biko, Rick: 85

Bill Haley (and His Comets): 112,
    170

Billy, Rev. Florian C.: 134

Blanchard, Jud: 187

Blishak, John "The Plow": 95, 215

Blossom, (Uncle) Jim: 128

Blossom, Blanche (Grandma
    Blossom): 16, 116-118, 126-129,
    169-170, 196, 201-203

Blossom, James F. "Jim" (Grandpa
    Blossom): 16, 116-118, 126, 128-
    129

Boardman, Gretchen: 88

Bogart, Bud: 44, 206

Bonds, Barry: 86

Boone, Pat: 113, 205

Bortnick, Martin: 25, 96, 175

Boswell, Daniel: 42

Bottino, Dennis: 134, 170, 175-177

Bowen, "Shorty": 95

Boyer, Clete: 77

Boyle, Huey: 42, 214

Boyle, Morey: 214

Bravi, Gerry: 96

Breese, Tom: 96

Brewer, Dave: 64, 150

Brewer, Gene: 30, 64

Brown, Harriet: 32

Brown, Jim: 128, 184

Brown, Paul L.: 134

Brunner, John R.: 153

Bundy, Harlow: 75

Buran, Frank: 141

Burt, Douglas Whiting: 153-154

Bush, George H.W.: 219

Cahill, Kevin: 64, 87, 150

Caldwell, Joseph A: 153

Campbell, Bobby: 140, 215

Carlini, Billy: 96

Carr, "Tonky": 43

Carr, Crème: 43

Carr, Donald: 43

Casella, P.J.: 234

Chamberlain, Wilt: 161

Charles, Ezzard: 80

Charsky, Steve: 132

Checker, Chubby: 112

Chernega, Dave: 95

Chetko, Penny: 87, 137, 204

Chipper, John: 168

Cider Mill: 90-91, 120

Ciotoli, Ed: 114, 143

Ciotoli, Mario: 96

Ciotoli, Tom Sr.: 90

Clark, Dick: 112

Coasters, The: 112, 205

Cobb, Harold V. "Ty": 34, 103, 129, 165, 182, 224

Colburn, Bobby: 123, 131-133, 154, 178, 184

Cole, Monte: 95, 145

Cole, Rob "Bubba": 96

Conklin, Larry: 85

Conrad, Joe: 122, 164

Consol, Dan "Cott": 95

Cook, Dave: 190

Cooke, Sam: 113

Corino, Arthur: 107

Corino, Marion: 224

Cosin, Fred: 130-131, 175

Costello, Lou: 102

Cousy, Bob: 160

Crampton, Bruce: 51, 174

Crawford, (brothers): 150

Crenshaw, Ben: 172

Crockett, Davy: 41

Crooks, Fran: 95

Crooks, Gary: 96

Crounse, Mike: 96

Crump, Ken: 150

Davis, Ernie: 151-152

Day Hollow Restaurant: 43-44, 47

Day, Doris: 138

Dearing, Chet: 206

Decker, Dave: 95

Decker, Ed "Duke": 96

Delaney, Raymond: 134

Dellos, John: 91, 114, 122, 155, 164-165, 179

Demkovich, Tom "Dink": 87

Derek, Bo: 138

Deyo, Bud: 187

Dibler, Patricia: 136-138

Diller, Henry "Hank": 121, 187

DiNunzio, Nick: 129, 165, 182

Dion and The Belmonts: 112

Dixon, F.W.: 119

Dobrovolsky, Anthony: 107

Dove, "Harky": 96

Downing, Alfonso: 102

Doyle, Barry: 190

Dudek, Tex: 171

Duster, William: 107

Dutcher, Dino: 96

Earp, Wyatt: 41

Ellis, Bruce: 175

Elton, John: 130

En-Joie Golf Club: 50-52, 171-174, 176, 188

En-Joie Park: 53, 55, 91, 102, 109, 119, 166, 170, 185, 199, 209-210, 212-215, 223, 232

Endicott, Henry B.: 18, 56, 106, 135, 152, 187, 193, 216, 229

Endicott-Johnson Corp: 16-20, 30, 32, 47, 50, 52, 68, 75-76, 82, 90, 105, 107, 109, 154, 167-168, 174, 184-185, 191, 194-196, 205-207, 210-211, 213, 221, 223-225, 228-235

Everly Brothers, The: 112, 205

Fabian: 114

Fabrizio, Mike: 96, 191

Fats Domino: 110, 112, 165

Feigner, Ed: 102

Felton, Kurt: 96

Ferris, Frank: 107

Ferris, Helen: 107

Fiori, James V.: 213

Fiori, Tino: 96

Fiori, Tom: 96, 103, 190-191

Floren, Myron: 112

Floyd, Raymond: 172

Fogarty, John: 160

Foli, Ed "Fols": 95

Ford, Whitey: 77, 98, 100

Fowler, Clarence: 171-174, 188

Fox, John W.: 95, 122

Foyt, A.J.: 157

Franklin, Burton: 47

Frechette, Lucille: 235

Frees, Paul: 49

Funicello, Annette: 125

Fusco, Gregrio "Gree": 210-211

Fusco, Mary: 211

Fusco, Tony: 115, 122

Gallagher, Bob: 95, 183

Gallaway, Fred: 107

Gance, Michael E.: 175

Gandhi, Mahatma: 177

Gargano, Bill R. Sr.: 95, 153, 187

Gault, Bill: 148

George, Armie: 96

George, Julius: 175

George, Keith: 233

Giarusso, Vincent: 175

Gifford, Frank: 126, 128

Gilroy, "Windy": 105-106

Giordano, Dr.: 47, 160

Giordano, Tom: 47, 60, 87, 150, 159-161, 175

Giordano, Vince: 160

Gipp, George "The Gipper": 220

Goodnow, Edward: 134, 175

Grant, Cary: 120

Green, Rev. John: 80, 117, 202

Grey Osterud, Nancy: 228-229

Grier, Roosevelt: 126

Grover's Pig Stand: 14, 118, 120, 144

Guarnieri, Mike: 96

Guccia, Bart "Goosh": 79, 95

Hallberg, George (Uncle George): 116, 127, 201-202

Hallberg, Margaret (Aunt Peg): 116, 127, 201-202

Hallberg, Richard: 202

Hambalek, Steve: 229, 234

Hamilton, Maurice "Hammy": 70, 96

Hanafin, Larry "Hondo": 96

Hanley, "Grandma" Grace: 95

Hanley, Jerry: 95

Hanley, Loftus: 96

Harder, Carl: 115

Harrelson, Ken "Hawk": 102

Hart, Johnny: 51, 132

Harter, Bob: 132

Harvey, Charles Wesley: 193

Havich, Richard: 25

Hawthorne, Helen: 31, 80

Herr, Lee: 168

A History of Endicott (James V. Fiori): 213

Hogan, Dan: 96

Hogan, Dom: 96

Hogan, Rich: 96

Hogan, Terry: 96

Hollister, Frederica "Fritz": 96

Holly, Buddy: 114

Hoover, Dick: 133, 135, 139-143, 183, 187

Hoover, Glenn: 142

Hotel Frederick: 107, 108-109, 173-174, 223

Hotel Mix: 107

Hover, Dick: 95, 190

Hover, Rick: 96

Hover, Steve: 96

Howard, Elston: 77

Hoyt, Frank "The Duke": 96

Hudock, Dr. John: 95

Hudson, Rock: 120

Huff, Sam: 126, 128

Huggins, Frank "Huggie": 44, 96, 175

Hughes, Bill "Doctor Mind": 96

Hurley, Tom: 187

Iacovazzi, Gary: 95

Iacovelli, Camilo: 39

IBM (International Business Machines): 32, 107, 154, 195, 199, 206, 215-216, 221-222, 224, 231-232

IBM Country Club: 75, 171

Ideal Hospital: 19, 52, 173-174

Innone, Anthony: 47

Jan & Dean: 205

Jaworski, Charlie: 182

Jennie F. Snapp Junior High School: 24, 26, 70, 85-90, 93, 97, 125, 137, 150, 161, 169, 204, 232

Jester, Brian "Juice": 96

Johannson, Ingemar: 100

Johnson, Capt. Francis A.: 107

Johnson, Charles F., Jr.: 206

Johnson, Frank A.: 233-234

Johnson, George F.: 17-18, 20, 34, 48-54, 56, 73-77, 79, 82, 90, 98, 100-101, 106-107, 118-119, 132, 134-135, 141, 152, 172-174, 176, 180, 187, 191-193, 195-196, 205-207, 209, 211-214, 216, 221-222, 225-232, 235

Johnson, George H.: 206

Johnson, George W.: 100

Julian, John: 130

Karaman, Fred: 60

Karl, Richie: 50, 51, 132, 174

Kazlauskas, Joe: 134, 175

Kehley, Todd: 191

Kelley, Todd "The Load": 96

Kendrick, Margot: 95

Kirdgus, Gene: 232

Kline, James: 153, 154

Klink, Bob: 94, 171

Koban, Ed "Fast Eddie": 79, 96, 103, 191

Kocak, Gerry: 115, 122

Kubek, Tony: 77

Kuhn, Tommy: 171

LaBare, Cyrill "Cy": 85-86

LaFuze, Maurice: 220

Lahar, Hal: 33, 97

Lawrence Welk Show, The: 112

Lea, Mom: 96

Lee, (Aunt) Alberta: 28, 211

Lee, (Aunt) Bessie: 36-37, 169

Lee, (Aunt) Honey: 28, 41, 82

Lee, Beatrice: 25, 28, 43, 61, 82, 88-89, 112, 120, 126, 150, 158, 167, 178, 203, 210, 212, 214

Lee, Bob: 28, 31, 36, 41, 45-47, 53, 80, 82, 207-208, 210, 211

Lee, Brenda: 114

Lee, Charles A. : 32

Lee, Charles Francis: 37, 207

Lee, Dan: 36, 41, 46, 210

Lee, Dora: 37, 207

Lee, Elizabeth: 37, 211

Lee, Erwin: 37, 207

Lee, Horace Jr.: 16-17, 26, 28, 31, 36, 39, 41-47, 53, 59-60, 64, 82, 100, 118, 120-122, 147-150, 160, 169, 178, 181, 203, 207, 210-211

Lee, Horace: 16, 31-32, 37-38, 41, 53-55, 79-81, 100-101, 117, 126, 147, 149, 157, 205-207, 210-212, 223

Lee, Jack: 28, 41, 44-46, 71, 204

Lee, Joe: 210

Lee, Lillian B. (Stanton): 16, 28, 30, 32, 37-38, 41, 53-55, 81, 117, 206-207, 211, 221, 223

Lee, Margaret "Aunt Maggie": 28, 36-39

Lee, Mayor E. Raymond: 130

Lee, Nancy: 28

Lee, Randall Howard "Randy": 120

Lee, Ray: 31, 36, 43, 45-47, 53, 82, 210

Lee, Richard: 28, 30, 43, 46

Lee, Robert Jr.: 211

Lee, Roberta: 28, 211

Lee, Rodney "Rod": 28, 58

Lee, Roger: 28, 30, 43, 46, 56

Lee, Sandra: 28

Lee, Sharon: 28, 211

Lee, Stewart: 28, 31-32, 36-41, 43, 45, 47, 65, 71, 81, 210

Legnini, Nick: 171

Lenkiewicz, Tony: 142
Letson, Carl: 69-70, 142
Levenson, Max: 195
Lewis, Jerry Lee: 111
Lewis, Jerry: 102
Liburdi, Ted: 122
Link, Edwin: 222
Liston, Sonny: 100
Little Richard: 112, 150
Lock, Don: 102
Logan, Johnny "Yachta": 51, 70, 132
Lollibridga, Gina: 138
"Lone Ranger": 41
Long, Dale: 77
Longo, Mike "Moose": 96
Loomis, Mary V.: 24, 232
Lopez, Hector: 77
Lord, Mr. & Mrs. Chester B.: 214
Loren, Sophia: 138
Loudon, Chuck "Chuckie Cheese": 96
Lucia, Joe: 95
Luciano, Ron "Loosh": 51, 132
Machalek, Dave: 96, 103, 127
Macon, Ronnie: 44, 127
Makowski, Matt: 44
Mantle, Mickey "The Mick": 54, 70, 72, 77, 79, 100
Maris, Roger: 77, 79
Marsh, Jason: 96
Marsh, John: 171
Marsh, Tim: 96
Martgetanski, John: 103
Martin, Dean "Rochester": 102
Marzo, Joe: 95
Mason, Tom: 95, 145
Mathyas, George: 150

Mays, Willie: 100
McLean, Richard: 95, 183, 190
McManus, Donald L: 153
Menichetti, Ron: 78
Mercereau, Dudley S.: 152, 154
Mercereau, Lawrence: 89
Michael, Jim: 130, 179
Miller, Marvin: 49
Miller, Mike: 96
Mills, Tom: 96
Mitchell, Chuck: 62, 87, 150
Mitchell, Pat "Pat Michell's": 15, 120, 140, 144
Montross, Bill: 142
Moore, Archie: 80
Moore, Rodney: 60
Moresco, Joe: 133, 183, 187
Morley, Al: 171
Morris, Lou: 96
Morris, Tom: 71, 87, 150
Mott, Joe: 96, 163
Muir, Bobby: 71, 87, 89, 123, 142, 150, 184
Mullins, Tom "Mully": 96
Munley, Paul Jr.: 96
Munley, Paul: 183
Murphy, Audie: 73
Murphy, Dan: 142-143, 202
Murtha, Mickey: 79, 95, 215
Musial, Stan "The Man": 101
Nalevanko, Mike: 60, 175
Nejeschleba, Joe: 122
Nelson, Ricky: 113
Nelson, Willie: 162
Newfrock, Jim: 191
Nicosia, Russ: 94-95, 99, 169, 190
Niles, Jerry: 122, 155, 175

Norris, Bobbie: 95, 163
Norris, Paul: 96, 123, 164
Norton, Gil: 131
Nowicki, Dr. Ted: 95
O'Reilly, (Coach) Gordie: 104, 187
Orbison, Roy: 112
Osbourne, Bob "Ozzie": 95
Pacioni, Ken: 91, 121-122, 136, 164
Padbury, Earl E.: 108
Palmer, Arnold: 51, 172
Paniccia, Vince: 96
Parkhurst, C. Burdette: 224
Parvin, Curt: 96
Pasquale, Tom: 96
Paterno, Joe: 215
Patkin, Max: 101
Patterson, Floyd: 80, 100
Pedley, Al: 95, 96
Pedley, Kerry: 96
Pemberton, Delbert: 134
Pepitone, Joe: 98, 100
Perfetti, :Tony 26
Perfetti, Laurene: 26, 34, 64, 87-89,
    99, 124-126, 137, 169, 204
Pettit, Bob: 54, 160
Picciano, "Bucky": 95
Picciano, Louis N.: 185
Pickering, Bill: 130, 145-146, 154,
    165, 179
Pilarcek, Jeff: 96
Pinto, John: 95
Pisani, Dom: 95
Pisani, Joe: 95
Pitkin, Mary L.: 96
Plaisted, Ed: 95
Plimpton, Bill: 187
Plugh, Kevin: 142

Popelka, Vito: 93, 96
Presley, Elvis: 112, 205
Prusia, Ben: 96
Prusia, Greg: 96
Pugh, Dick: 115, 143, 178-179
Randesi, Jeanne: 136, 138
Rando, Chris: 96
Reagan, Jerry: 154
Reagan, Ronald: 216, 219-225
Rejda, Ron: 96, 216
Richardson, Bobby: 77, 163
Rita, Alex: 96
Rivers, Johnny: 114, 170
Rizzuto, Phil: 77
Robbins, Mrs.: 170
Roberto, Joe: 95
Robertson, Oscar "The Big O": 54,
    160
Robin Hood: 41
Robinson, "Sugar Ray": 80
Robinson, Mel: 133
Robistelli, Andy: 126
Rockne, Knute: 220
Rogers, G. Tracey: 193
Rogers, Roy: 41
Roma, Felix: 61
Romeo, Tony: 95
Rose, Tony: 96
Rosencrance, Roy: 46, 211
Rossi, Al: 61, 150
Rossi, Dave: 30, 64
Rucker, Cal: 187
Samiani, Nino: 96
Sammon, Dave: 78, 114, 133, 143,
    154-155, 179, 184
Scott, Roberta: 175
Sedaka, Neil: 112

Sergi, Marie: 15

Sergi, Sam: 15, 47, 68

Shady, Josephine "Josie": 87, 137, 175, 204

Shannon, Del: 113

Shawkey, John: 78

Shepherd, Bob: 198

Shields, Jarvis: 96, 123, 164

Sick, Adona: 106, 175

Sindelar, Joey: 172

Sipko, Dave: 175

Skowron, Bill "Moose": 77

Smith, Bob: 131, 175

Snead, "Slammin'" Sammy: 171

Soltis, Wendall: 153

Sorochinsky, Frank "Sarge": 45, 95, 175, 177

Southworth, Norma: 175

Spadine, Lee: 96

Stanton, Ray: 115

Starring, Bill: 132

Steenburg, Pat: 87, 137, 204

Stone, Mike: 60, 150, 159

Streno, Dick: 122, 127, 164

Summerall, Pat: 126

Swayze, John Cameron: 127

Sweet, Lillian (Johnson): 213

Sylvester, "Slim": 161, 185

Tatko, Ken: 96

Terenzi, Len: 102

Testa, Dick: 96

Thayer, Bill: 142, 150, 175

Thurber, Egbert A.: 33

Tidick, Wayne "T": 96

Tingley, Bob: 30, 64

Tingley, Joe: 87

Tittle, Y.A.: 126-127

Tovornik, Bernadette: 175

Trevino, "Super Max" Lee: 171

Truillo, Jim: 95

Turner, "Red": 143

Turner, (Aunt) Harriet: 28, 45, 206

Turner, Bernard "Uncle Bun": 28, 45-46, 53, 143, 202

Turver, Charles: 93, 138, 174

Twain, Mark: 151

Ty Cobb Stadium: 60, 63, 78, 90, 97, 103, 131-132, 142, 154, 162, 168, 170, 181, 183, 185, 189, 197-198, 216, 218-220, 222

Union-Endicott High School: 18, 26, 30, 33, 92-93, 96, 106, 137, 138, 168, 217, 231, 232

Unitas, Johnny: 54

Valachovic, Tony: 96

Van Wieren, Pete: 102

Vanderpool, Lee: 87

Veruto, Bob: 96

Vetter, Hank: 95

Villanti, John: 95

Villanti, Peggy: 95

Villanti, Steve: 96

Vivona, Dick: 115

Vivona, Rich: 181

Wahila, Anne Marie: 131, 175

Wallace, George C.: 176

Wallace, George: 114-115, 178

Ward, Zack: 43

Washington Avenue "The Avenue": 19, 22, 33, 47, 52-53, 56, 61, 70, 82, 91, 93, 103, 105-109, 111, 113, 119, 130, 134, 140, 144, 153, 158, 165, 168, 170, 173, 175, 179, 184, 193-195, 199,

Washington Avenue "The Avenue" (continued): 205, 212, 215-217, 223, 232

Waters, Chris "Muddy": 79, 96, 103, 164

Watson, Thomas J. Jr.: 73

Watson, Thomas J. Sr.: 73, 75-77, 79, 132, 141, 152, 187, 221-222, 231

Watson, Tom: 172

Watts, John: 142

Wayne, John: 120

Webster, Alex: 126

Webster, Daniel: 90

Wesko, Mike Sr.: 95

West, Jerry: 161

West, Linneaus W.: 42

West, Martin: 42

West, Orman: 42

Wheeler, Bob: 103

Wilson, Markus: 96, 123, 164

Witter, Patty: 138

Wolf, Dave: 96, 191

Wood, Natalie: 138

Working Lives (Nancy Grey Osterud): 228

Wurtenburg, Bob: 60, 95, 190

Yeager, Howard: 68

Yum Yum Corner: 44, 47

Zades, James: 107

Zappia, Fred Jr.: 79

Zappia, Fred Sr.: 61, 95

Zimmerman, Dr. Bill: 96

Zonio, Carl: 134, 175

"Zorro": 41

Zur, Charlie: 96

Zur, Louise: 96

Zur, Randy: 79, 95, 103

Zur, Rod: 190